Sources
for a Biography of
SHAKESPEARE

BY

E. K. CHAMBERS

OXFORD
AT THE CLARENDON PRESS
1946

OXFORD UNIVERSITY PRESS
AMEN HOUSE, E.C. 4
London Edinburgh Glasgow New York
Toronto Melbourne Cape Town Bombay
Calcutta Madras
GEOFFREY CUMBERLEGE
PUBLISHER TO THE UNIVERSITY

PRINTED IN GREAT BRITAIN AT THE UNIVERSITY PRESS, OXFORD
BY JOHN JOHNSON, PRINTER TO THE UNIVERSITY

PREFATORY NOTE

THIS booklet records the substance and often preserves the language of a course of lectures given to students working for the Bachelorship of Letters at Oxford during 1929 to 1938. The order of the topics has been somewhat altered, and I have not refrained from making use of a little material which was not available at the time of the lectures. These were concerned with Shakespeare's personal life only, and did not, except incidentally, touch upon the problems of his theatrical career.

CONTENTS

INTRODUCTORY

SHAKESPEARE'S personal life is made the subject of these lectures, less for its own sake, than as typical. The study of it began in the eighteenth century with the edition (1709) of Nicholas Rowe. He was followed by Samuel Johnson, George Steevens, Edward Capell, Isaac Reed, and George Chalmers, but most successfully by Edmund Malone (1741–1812), whose latest results were published in 1821 by James Boswell in what is called the *Third Variorum Shakespeare*.

Modern scholarship has, of course, made use of and added a good deal to these earlier attempts. There are Lives of Shakespeare, such as those by Sir Sidney Lee and J. Q. Adams, which mainly take the form of a continuous narrative, but do not set out *in extenso* the original documents on which they are based. These are summarized and subjective interpretations added, from the writer's sense of probability and general knowledge of Elizabethan conditions. Such books have their value, but the scholar wants to go behind them. And, however carefully the work is done, he will find that some of the summaries do not represent the sources with precision, and that some of the subjective inferences are too confident. It is the first lesson, never to be content with a second-hand statement when a first-hand source is available.

The sources, so far as known to him, were fully set out by J. O. Halliwell-Phillips in his *Outlines of the Life of Shakespeare*, which took its final form in 1887. It is a useful, but rather ill-arranged and imperfectly indexed work. My own *William Shakespeare, A Study of Facts and Problems* (1930) attempts to be both a Life and a collection of sources. I have made some additions in *Shakespearean Gleanings* (1944).

But I must warn you to beware of my subjectivity as well as that of others. Even since 1930 some additions have been made to our knowledge, especially by Professor Leslie Hotson in his *Shakespeare versus Shallow* (1931) and *I, William Shakespeare* (1937). There may be still possibilities to be explored, often involving laborious and perhaps disappointing research. But, for the reason of the long pains that have been spent upon it, a survey of the ground covered in the case of Shakespeare will help to show the kind of material likely to be available for any comparable biography.

Some preliminary classification of the various types of source is desirable. We shall have to consider in their turn (*a*) Records, (*b*) Contemporary Literary Allusions, in the writings of men other than Shakespeare himself, (*c*) Traditions emerging at dates after his lifetime, and (*d*) Inferences, sometimes fond imaginings, from his own works.

RECORDS

RECORDS will take most of our time, and of these we will attempt a sub-classification, according to the custody in which they once were, and in some cases may still be found. Every man, not completely illiterate, commits himself during his lifetime to the writing of letters or other documents, sometimes of a legal character. They may pass to others, either at the time of writing, or, if he preserves them himself, after his death. They become records of his career. But man, being a social animal, is throughout his life linked up with institutions. He holds a house and lands, in accordance with legal provisions. He is a member of a church. He is educated at a school and perhaps a university. He dwells in a village or town community. He follows a profession or occupation. He is the subject of a state. And in all these capacities, which among them affect most of the actions of his life, he is in touch with institutions and organizations, which themselves keep records of transactions in which he is concerned. They are not, of course, all preserved, or easily accessible. That is where research comes in.

We shall have, therefore, to consider, in their turn, Tenurial, Ecclesiastical, Municipal, Occupational, Court, National (subdivided as Administrative and Legal), and finally more Personal Records. And, as the relations of men with other men, or with institutions, are bilateral, records may overlap. One end of a transaction may be here, the other there.

AN OUTLINE

LET us at this point bear in mind the main features of Shakespeare's life—by anticipation of course, and merely as a convenient scaffolding, since the statements to be made are themselves largely based upon existing records. We will not attempt to go into the history of his plays.

He was born in 1563 or early 1564, the son of John Shakespeare of Henley Street, Stratford-on-Avon, and his wife Mary Arden. He married Anne Hathaway in November 1582. A daughter Susanna was baptized at Stratford on 26 May 1583, and twins Hamnet and Judith on 2 February 1585. Hamnet was buried at Stratford in 1596.

Stratford, from very early days, had been part of the great landed domain of the Bishops of Worcester, and in the first half of the sixteenth century the Bishop still held two manors there. One was known as Stratford Burgus, and in it had been established during the thirteenth century a Gild of Holy Cross, which did much for the welfare of the inhabitants, maintaining, besides its own chapel, an almshouse and a free school. To the south of it lay Stratford Vetus, which apparently included parts of the agricultural villages of Shottery and Welcombe. Here were the parish church, which was common to both manors, and a College of priests, who served it and held the tithes. In 1547 both Gild and College were dissolved under the *Chantries Act*. In 1549 the Bishop was forced by the Crown to transfer his manors to John Dudley, Earl of Warwick, and later Duke of Northumberland. On his attainder in 1553 they reverted to the Crown, which held them until 1562, when they were granted to Northumberland's son Ambrose Dudley, Earl of Warwick. On his death in 1590, they again reverted to the Crown, and were sold to Sir Edward Greville of Milcote. But in 1553 the position of Stratford Burgus as a self-governing community had been established by a royal charter of incorporation, which, while preserving the rights of the lord of the manor, set up a Council of aldermen and capital burgesses under an elected bailiff, with power to acquire property, to make statutes and ordinances for the well-being of the town, and to hold a Court of Record for disputes and debts not involving more than £30. It was to have the tithes, and was charged with the salaries of a vicar and the master of the free school.

There were many Shakespeares in Warwickshire during the sixteenth century. The earliest to make his appearance in Stratford was a John in 1533. He was not the poet's father, who was almost certainly the John Shakespeare of Snitterfield *agricola*, who in 1561 administered the estate there of his late father Richard, long a tenant of Robert Arden, whose daughter John married. In Snitterfield records Richard is also sometimes called Shakstaff and Shakeschafte. This John first makes his appearance at Stratford in 1552, when he was fined for having an unauthorized dung-hill in Henley Street. In 1590 he had two contiguous houses in the same street, now known as the Birthplace and the Woolshop. He is described as a glover in 1592, but tradition makes him also a wool-dealer. For some years he prospered in business, and in 1568 he became bailiff. But about 1577 he seems to have fallen into financial difficulties, and ceased to take part in town affairs. In 1601 he died. His will, if he made one, is unknown. But his two houses in Henley Street were later owned by the poet. A third John Shakespeare, traceable in Stratford from about 1586 to 1595, was a corvisor or shoemaker.

Tradition reports that William Shakespeare left Stratford at an early age, as the result of a deer-stealing exploit in the park of Sir Thomas Lucy at Charlecote. It is possible that he is to be identified with a William Shakeshafte, who in 1581 was a player in a company maintained by one Alexander Houghton of Lea in Lancashire, and was commended in Houghton's will to Sir Thomas Hesketh of Rufford, in the same county. If so, William may have been using the variant of his grandfather's name, which has already been noted. Sir Thomas Hesketh had in fact players in 1587, and his relations with the Stanleys, Earls of Derby, make it not unlikely that on his death in or about 1588 Shakeshafte passed into the service of Ferdinando Lord Strange, who himself became Earl in 1593. Of Lord Strange's players there are many records. Through them William may easily have gone on into the London theatrical world, where he is found in 1592, writing probably for Lord Pembroke's men, and called by the envious Robert Greene 'the only Shake-scene in a countrey'. This is of course conjecture. Wherever Shakespeare was during these formative years, the baptisms of his children and the fact that he became a party to a business transaction of his father's in 1587 show that he was not wholly out of touch with Stratford. Elizabethan players travelled widely, and they are found at Stratford as elsewhere, although Strange's are not in fact named in the extant records of that town.

From 1592 onwards Shakespeare's head-quarters were doubtless in or near London. We find him living in 1595 at St. Helen's, Bishopsgate, in 1599 at the Clink on the Southwark Bankside in Surrey, and in 1604 or later in Cripplegate. A statement by John Aubrey that he once lived at Shoreditch lacks confirmation. In 1613 he bought a house in the Blackfriars, but this may have been only an investment. He still had it in 1616, but one John Robinson was living there. His connexion with Stratford, if he ever broke it, was resumed in 1597, when he bought the considerable house of New Place in Chapel Street ward. This, however, he let to Thomas Greene, who in 1609 expected to be able to continue his tenancy for another year. Some other local purchases followed in 1602. At the time of his death he had also his father's two houses in Henley Street. He made his will on 25 March 1616, leaving his houses and other property to his daughter Susanna, a money bequest to his daughter Judith, and to his wife, who would be entitled under common law to her jointure, his second-best bed. On 23 April 1616 he died. Judith, a few months before, had married Thomas Quiney. She had three sons, who all died early. Susanna, in 1607, had married John Hall, of a Middlesex family, who became a physician, and settled in Stratford, where he dwelt after his father-in-law's death at New Place. He died in 1635 and Susanna in 1649. They had a daughter Elizabeth, who married firstly Thomas Nash, and secondly John, later Sir John, Bernard. Both occupied New Place. Elizabeth had no children, and on her death in 1670 Shakespeare's family became extinct. Shadows we are, and shadows we pursue.

And now we may turn to the Records. Let us recall the classification of them, already given, as Tenurial, Ecclesiastical, Municipal, Occupational, Court, National (subdivided as Administrative and Legal), and finally Personal Records.

TENURIAL RECORDS

LAND and houses, in Shakespeare's day, were held by grant or lease, either from the Crown or from the lord of a manor. There were two forms of granted tenure. One was called 'freehold' or in a borough 'burgage', the other 'copyhold', because the evidence for it was a 'copy' given to the tenant of an entry in a manorial court-roll. A manorial holding might be subject to certain dues, such as a quit-rent, or an obligation to attend as a juryman in the lord's court. Property, so acquired, might be bought and sold, or sublet, by a signed deed of conveyance, or, in the case of copyhold, by a symbolical act of delivery in the court. It might pass also under a bequest or marriage settlement, or by inheritance to the next of kin. The evidences of ownership are called 'title-deeds'. They are naturally preserved with care, and go to the new holder, when the property is alienated.

Several of Shakespeare's title-deeds are known. We have noted that in 1587 he was concerned with a business affair of his father's. This related to a house and land, the property of his mother. There is no evidence that they ever passed to William. At the time of his death he had his father's two houses in Henley Street at Stratford, but whether by bequest or as next of kin we cannot tell. John Shakespeare's will, if he made one, is not preserved.

William's own first known purchase was of New Place, a burgage of the manor of Stratford, which he bought

about 1597 from William Underhill. No deed of conveyance is known. But here we have an example of that overlapping between a man's own records and those of an
institution, which we have already noted. It was cus-
tomary to supplement a deed of conveyance by a suit
brought by the purchaser against the vendor in a High
Court, that of Common Pleas. It was merely formal. There
was no actual conflict. The suit ended by the admission
of the vendor that the property was the purchaser's. This
was recorded in a decision of the court, known technically
as a 'fine', in the sense of a *finis* or end of suit. A 'copy' or
'exemplification' of this was given to each of the parties,
and a third, called a 'foot of fine' remained among the
court archives. The object was for greater security of
record than documents in individual hands could give.
The foot of fine for the purchase of New Place is still in the
Record Office, and one of the exemplifications, probably
the purchaser's, is in the Shakespeare's Birthplace Museum
at Stratford. Oddly enough, there was a second suit in
the Court of Common Pleas during 1602, probably because
the vendor's estate had been forfeited to the Crown for the
felony of murder, and regranted to his brother, and Shakespeare's legal advisers thought a second transfer to him
desirable. Of this fine the foot and both exemplifications
are preserved. The former is also in the Record Office,
the latter were found among papers of a Severne family
at Wallop in Shropshire. They are now in the Folger
Collection at Washington.

In 1602 Shakespeare bought from Walter Getley a copyhold cottage standing in Chapel Street, also called Walker's
Street and Dead Lane, at Stratford. It was not, however,
held from the manor of Stratford, but from that of Row-
ington in north Warwickshire. The 'copy' is at the Birthplace. A 'fine' was not usual on the transfer of copyhold.

In the same year he also bought from William and John Combe 107 acres of freehold agricultural land in that part of the manor of Stratford Vetus known as Welcombe, together with appurtenances, apparently including twenty acres of pasture, and with common rights of grazing over the open fields of which the land formed a part. In this case we have, at the Birthplace, a conveyance signed by the vendors and endorsed with a witnessed note of delivery to Shakespeare's brother Gilbert on his behalf, and also, among the Common Pleas records, the foot of a fine entered into, for some reason, at the much later date of 1610.

The purchase shows Shakespeare, already by 1602, in a position to make a fairly substantial investment. This was emphasized in 1605 by his acquisition of a moiety of certain ecclesiastical tithes falling due in the parish of Stratford, including those on corn and hay in Old Stratford, Welcombe, and Bishopton. The history of the Stratford tithes is rather complicated. The ownership had once belonged to the College of Stratford. In 1544 its Warden, Anthony Barker, had granted a lease of them to William Barker, presumably a kinsman. On the dissolution of the College in 1547 the ownership passed to the Crown, which transferred it to the borough by the incorporation charter of 1553. The lease remained with the Barkers. In 1580 John Barker gave a sublease to Sir John Huband, who died in 1583, leaving one moiety to his brother Ralph, who sold it to Shakespeare, and the other to Lady Digby, who in 1596 further sublet it to William Combe. He was apparently acting for his nephew Thomas Combe, on whose death in 1609 it passed to his son, a second William Combe.

Shakespeare's interests in Welcombe caused him some trouble during the latter part of his life. In 1611 he was party to a Chancery action to secure the payment by

William Combe of his share of the rental of the tithes due to the Barker family under the sublease of 1580, failure in which might lead to a re-entry of them into occupation. Combe, however, acknowledged his liability. Another complication arose in 1614 through a scheme promoted by one William Replingham and one Arthur Mainwaring, and supported by Combe, for the enclosure of the open fields of Welcombe. This Shakespeare seems to have thought likely to be detrimental to his interests, both as a tithe-holder and as a land-holder. The Corporation also, as the ultimate tithe-owners, were hostile, and careful notes of the proceedings were kept by Thomas Greene, the steward of the borough and clerk to its Court of Record. So far as Shakespeare was concerned, he seems to have been satisfied as regards his tithes by an agreement with Replingham to secure him against loss, and as regards his land by learning that the enclosure would not affect that part of the fields in which it lay. In fact the enclosure, owing to the opposition of the Corporation, was never carried out. It was stayed by orders of the Judges of Assize in 1615, 1616, and 1617, and finally by the Privy Council in 1619. The affair does not appear to have disturbed Shakespeare's relations with the Combe family. William's uncle John had left him £5 in 1614, and to William's brother Thomas he left his sword in 1616. Tradition, as we shall see, has something more to say about Shakespeare and the Combes. The conveyance to Shakespeare of the tithes lease and a contemporary copy of his articles with Replingham are at the Birthplace, and among the records of the Corporation of Stratford are a bond from Huband to observe the covenants of the lease, the draft Bill of Complaint in Chancery with Combe's answer, and the Town Clerk's notes of Shakespeare's holding in Welcombe, and of the enclosure controversy.

One other investment by Shakespeare was not in Stratford, but in London. Here he bought in 1613 a house standing in part over the gateway of what had once been the Priory of Blackfriars. This had been dissolved in 1547, and the house granted to Sir Francis Bryan. It passed through various hands to one Mathias Bacon, and from him to one Henry Walker, who sold it to Shakespeare. He does not appear to have ever occupied it. At the time of his death it was the residence of one John Robinson. Here we get a good example of the bilateral character of legal transactions. Conveyances were often executed in duplicate. The vendor signed one and gave it to the purchaser. The purchaser signed another and gave it to the vendor. In this case both documents are preserved. The vendor's signature is on one in the Folger Library at Washington, the purchaser's on another in the London Guildhall. An enrolment of the former is among the Chancery Close Rolls. After the purchase Shakespeare mortgaged back the house to Walker, probably until the purchase-money was ready. The mortgage-deed is in the British Museum. Finally, in 1615, Shakespeare and others brought a Complaint in Chancery for the recovery of muniments relating to the whole Blackfriars estate. These were still held by Mathias Bacon, and the Chancery records contain an order for the delivery of them in court. The fact of Shakespeare's acquisition was known from the Close Roll, before the original conveyances were discovered. This illustrates the greater security of institutional records as compared with more personal ones.

ECCLESIASTICAL RECORDS

TITHES were of course an ecclesiastical affair, but Shakespeare, as a leaseholder, was not concerned with the purposes to which his rent was put. After the dissolution of the college, the tithes had been granted to the Corporation, who were charged with the maintenance of the free school. It is likely enough that Shakespeare was educated at it, but of this we have no evidence beyond tradition. He is not traceable at either university.

The Vicar of Stratford kept a register of baptisms, marriages, and burials, which is still preserved there, although the entries up to 1600 are only in a transcript. They begin in 1558, and record, amongst other events in John Shakespeare's family, the baptisms of William himself, of his brothers and sisters, and of his children Susanna, Hamnet, and Judith. Here, too, are the marriages of Susanna and Judith, and the burials of all three children and of William's widow Anne. In the church of Stratford are his tombstone, with an elaborate monument, and those of Anne and Susanna. What is notably missing is the record in any parochial register of William's own marriage. It is possible, as we shall see, that it was at Temple Grafton, five miles from Stratford, for which no contemporary parochial register is known to exist. The will of Alexander Houghton (1581), which mentions William Shakeshafte, is in the Ecclesiastical Court of Chester.

Much responsibility for the observance of ecclesiastical law in Warwickshire rested with the Bishop of Worcester, in whose diocese it lay. He had officials at his disposal. A registrar kept for him a record of licences granted to teachers, or for marriages to be solemnized without the full normal preliminary of banns. The Register is now preserved in the Edgar Tower at Worcester, and in it is an entry of the issue of such a licence for the marriage of Shakespeare. It is dated on 27 November 1582, six months only before the baptism of Shakespeare's daughter Susanna. Some of the documents needed to justify the Bishop in giving the licence are missing, but there remains, also in the Edgar Tower, a bond given by two sureties on the bridegroom's behalf to hold the Bishop harmless for allowing the ceremony to take place on a single asking of the banns. Unfortunately there is a discrepancy between the two documents. The licence describes the bride as Anne Whateley of Temple Grafton and the bond as Anne Hathwey of Stratford. The facts remain a little obscure, but it is probable that she was an Anne Hathaway, neither of Temple Grafton nor of Stratford, but of Shottery, although the marriage may possibly, for some reason, have taken place at Temple Grafton, the register of which, for the period concerned, is not preserved.

Minor breaches of ecclesiastical discipline were dealt with by archdeacons during tours of the diocese. For graver ones the Bishop had a more important official than the Registrar in his Vicar General or Chancellor, himself an ecclesiastic learned in canon law, who presided over a Consistory Court in the cathedral. Several muniments of this court are preserved in the Edgar Tower at Worcester, a Visitation Book for matters disposed of locally, an Act Book for more important ones dealt with at head-quarters, a Deposition Book for the evidence of witnesses. The surviving Visitation Book does not cover the period of Shakespeare's early life, but records an excommunication of his daughter Judith and Thomas Quiney in 1616 for marrying without licence during a prohibited season. In the Act Book is a suit of 1613 brought by his other daughter Susanna against one John Lane for defamation of her moral character. The Consistory Court dealt also with the probate of wills. Shakespeare's, however, was not proved in the Worcester diocese, but in London, under the superior jurisdiction of the Archbishop of Canterbury, and is now in the Principal Probate Register at Somerset House. It consists of three sheets in an English hand, probably that of a clerk of the solicitor who drafted it, and containing many corrections and interlineations. Each sheet bears Shakespeare's signature. An endorsement by a commissary shows that it was admitted to probate in this condition, on the oath of one of the executors. This is followed by the note *Inventorium exhibitum*. But the actual inventory of Shakespeare's property is not preserved.

One other ecclesiastical document is of an exceptional character. In 1591, during the recurrent scare of a Spanish invasion, county commissioners were appointed to collect and report to the Privy Council the names of persons who did not attend church monthly, and thus brought themselves under suspicion of being Catholic recusants, likely to give support to the enemy. A list of 1592 for Stratford, among the *Greville Papers* at Warwick Castle, includes the name of John Shakespeare, but a note by the commissioners adds, as regards him and several others, that the reason for their absence was believed to be the fear of process for debt, which in the sixteenth century might involve an arrest even on a Sunday.

MUNICIPAL RECORDS

MANY of the records of Stratford still exist, and are now housed in the Birthplace. They include the minutes of meetings of the Corporation, the accounts of the Chamberlains, who were its financial officers, and the proceedings of the Court of Record, which had a jurisdiction over financial disputes, not involving over £30. With them are many miscellaneous documents, some of which are of a non-official character, such as the notebook of Thomas Greene, Steward to the Corporation, and some letters of the Quiney family, into which Judith Shakespeare married. Others, of a similar type, have found their way into the Folger Collection at Washington and elsewhere. There is a good deal on John Shakespeare, but little on William, which is at least negative evidence that he stood aloof from local affairs.

With his purchase of New Place in 1597 we have already dealt. He does not appear in the Corporation Minutes. The Chamber accounts for 1598 record a payment to him of 10d. for a load of stone, those of 1614 a payment for sack and claret given to a preacher at New Place. We may infer that, at least once in his life, Shakespeare heard a sermon. About 1604 he brought an action in the Court of Record against one Phillip Rogers for the sum of £1. 15s. 10d., the price of some malt, and in 1608–9 another against John Addenbrooke and his surety Thomas Horneby for a debt of £6 and the costs of recovery. Some of the miscellaneous documents also refer to New Place. In 1598 Shakespeare is noted in a return of corn and malt as having ten quarters there. In September 1609 Thomas Greene was hoping to have another year's occupation of the house. A lease of neighbouring property, at some time between 1603 and 1616, refers to it as bounded on the west by 'Mr William Shaxpeare of Pynley Holt'. But there is an error here. It was the property leased, not Shakespeare's, which had once belonged to the priory of Pinley. An inventory of the goods of one Robert Johnson shows that he held a barn of Shakespeare from the poet in 1611. This seems to be the only reference to his Henley Street property before the date of his will. In the same year he contributed towards the expense of prosecuting a Bill in Parliament for the better repair of the highways. Richard Quiney's correspondence of 1598 deals with attempts to borrow money from Shakespeare, and also to persuade him to invest in the Corporation's tithes. This, however, has no obvious connexion with his actual lease of tithes in 1605. The municipal records of London, although valuable on the history of the theatres, do not seem to contain anything personal to Shakespeare. Here, too, there are many subsidiary documents, which may not have been exhaustively studied. But human time and energy are limited.

OCCUPATIONAL RECORDS

DETAILS as to the succession of Shakespeare's plays, and as to the theatres at which they were given, will not fall within the scope of these lectures. Something, however, must be said about his status as a player within the national community. Occupations, in the England of the sixteenth and seventeenth centuries, were still largely organized in gilds. The ordinances of these, which were to some extent under control by the civic corporations, contained regulations for the quality of the goods sold, for the training of apprentices, and especially for the limitation of numbers admitted to their rolls. The freemanship of a gild was normally acquired either by paternity or by apprenticeship. John Shakespeare, for example, was a member of the Gild of Glovers and Whittawers of Stratford. There was, however, no Gild of Actors in London. Some of them may have belonged to the Gild of Musicians, or by patrimony or earlier occupation to other gilds. And when plays came to be printed they fell within the scope of the

Gild of Stationers and were recorded in a register, kept by them.

The members of an acting company were linked together in two ways. Firstly they were partners in a business enterprise. This was constituted by a deed, known as a 'composition'. Each member gave a bond to carry out its terms, contributed to the stock of properties, for which he was allowed on retirement, and had a right to a share in the takings, which were divided at frequent intervals. But not all the takings. Others, apparently the entrance fees to some or all of the galleries, were set aside as rent to the owners of the playhouse. These might be either outside capitalists or an inner ring of the more well-to-do members of the company, who are sometimes called the house-keepers. This appears from the records of various lawsuits, for players, like other Elizabethans, were a litigious folk. We have not a 'composition' for any of Shakespeare's companies, but we have records of the shares which he held in the Globe and the Blackfriars, although we do not know when, or to whom, he parted with them. They are not specified in his will. To the nature of the lawsuits we shall come later.

The second link was one of patronage. Apart from certain troops of boys, which had developed from the choirs of cathedrals or royal chapels, and with which we are not concerned, each company had a 'lord' or 'patron'. This was generally, in the case of a London company, some nobleman prominent at Court. In a sense they were his household servants. They wore his livery and badge. It does not appear that they had wages, but if they gave a performance before him they would get a 'reward'. For the most part, however, they were able to play for their own profit in their theatres, or on country tours, where their relation to their lord saved them from the severe restrictions imposed by Elizabethan legislation upon vagrants. They carried with them a letter of recommendation from their lord, but also, in Shakespeare's time, a licence from an officer of the royal household, known as the Master of the Revels.

We cannot be sure in what companies Shakespeare began his career as an actor and playwright. If he is to be identified with the William Shakeshafte of 1581, he may have passed successively from that of Alexander Houghton, to those of Sir Thomas Hesketh, Ferdinando Stanley, Lord Strange, afterwards Earl of Derby, and possibly Henry Herbert, Earl of Pembroke. But we first find him clearly, from the autumn of 1594 onwards, in that of two successive Lords Hunsdon, Henry and George Carey, father and son, each of whom, with a short interval between them, held the post of Lord Chamberlain in Queen Elizabeth's Household. This lasted to the accession of James the First in 1603, when a considerable change took place. The chief London companies were now granted the direct patronage of the King and his family. The Lord Chamberlain's men became the King's men, and their licence from the Master of the Revels was replaced by a patent from the Crown. This brings us to a new group of Records, that of the Court.

COURT RECORDS

THE organization of the Royal Household was an elaborate one. There were three great officers. The Lord Steward supervised the Hall, the Kitchen, and other offices of provision. The Lord Chamberlain, with Gentlemen, Ushers, and Grooms of the Chamber under him, was responsible for the upstairs department, the Great Chamber, where receptions were held, the Queen's or King's private apartments, the Bedchamber, the Revels, the Wardrobe, and the like. The Master of the Horse looked after the Stables.

Actors fell within the Lord Chamberlain's department, and Shakespeare and his fellows were sworn to the royal service as Grooms in Ordinary of the Chamber, without fee. Without fee, but also without normal duties of attendance. They remained at liberty to continue playing for gain at their theatres, the Globe, built for them in 1599, and the Blackfriars, which they obtained in addition a few years later. In both of these Shakespeare was a 'sharer' or 'housekeeper'. And if the company was called upon, as it often was, to present a play at Court it continued to receive, as it had done before it was attached to the Household, a special 'reward' which was payable by the Treasurer of the Chamber, an officer in the Lord Chamberlain's department. Unfortunately, few of the main records of this department, during Shakespeare's lifetime, are preserved to us. It is probable that many perished during a fire at Whitehall in 1619. It is regrettable, because the Lord Chamberlain exercised authority over disputes between members of the patented Companies, and the post-1619 records thus throw useful light on the later history of these. One such record does in fact help us about Shakespeare himself. In a dispute of 1635 the history of the Globe and Blackfriars theatres was recounted, with a mention of Shakespeare as a 'deserving man', who held shares in both houses. But for the actual period of his lifetime we have only accounts of expenditure rendered to the exchequer by subsidiary officers in the Lord Chamberlain's Department, and here Shakespeare, if named at all, only makes a brief and formal appearance.

There were three such subsidiary departments. The accounts of the Treasurer of the Chamber show Shakespeare acting as payee for the Company, then still

Lord Hunsdon's, in 1595, which suggests that he was already one of its leading members. They show him again as receiving, with others of his fellows, a special allowance in 1604, during an embassy of the Constable of Castile to negotiate for a peace with Spain, when the players seem to have been called upon, exceptionally, to do service as ordinary Grooms of the Chamber. In 1612–13 they name several of his plays as given at Court during the winter holidays. This also is, unfortunately, exceptional. As a rule the Treasurer of the Chamber only noted the number and not the names of the plays rewarded. He had no thought for us. A second subsidiary department of the Chamber was that of the Master of the Wardrobe, whose accounts for 1604 show Shakespeare and his fellows as each receiving four and a half yards of red cloth, to furnish liveries for the coronation of James I. A third was under the Master of the Revels. He, too, recorded annually his expenditure on setting forth the plays given at Court, for which he had to find scenery and properties, and in two years, although not regularly, he was good enough to provide a list of the plays performed. These lists have been the subject of much controversy. On the face of them they are of great value in determining the succession of Shakespeare's plays. But their authenticity has been more than once challenged. I have never myself believed that they were forgeries, and the suggestion seems now to have been finally disproved in an elaborate study by Mr. A. E. Stamp of the Record Office, well worth reading as an example of the complicated evidence, which has sometimes to be considered in determining such matters.

An organization, which was not strictly part of the Household, although related to it, was that of the College of Heralds. These had once been military officers, and were supervised by the Earl Marshal, still representing the Crown, as the traditional head of the army. They appeared in processions at a coronation, and at tilts. But their main function was now to superintend the honorific right to bear a coat of arms, which had ceased to be of military significance, but still conveyed a higher rank than that of an ordinary gentleman. Two drafts for grants of arms to John Shakespeare exist, one of 1596, the other of 1599, which added the right to impale the arms of Arden, the family of John's wife. Any such grant had, of course, to be made to John, as the living head of his house. But doubtless the real applicant was William. This emerges from a contemporary protest from heralds, other than those making the grants, who alleged that in this and other cases they had been conferred on base persons. In fact, however, John Shakespeare, who as bailiff of Stratford had also held offices under the Crown there, was perfectly entitled, in accordance with contemporary practice, to apply for a coat of arms. One of the grants must have been actually made, since the arms appear on the poet's monument and on his daughter's seal. There is, however, no evidence that he ever impaled those of Arden. An interesting point in the drafts is that they recite, as part of the justification for John's claim, a grant of lands and tenements in Warwickshire made to his parent, grandfather, or in one case great-grandfather, and late ancestor, in reward for services to Henry VII, of which there is no confirmation among the calendared records of that sovereign. But a contemporary chronicler tells us that it was the custom of the Heralds, in making grants to 'pretend antiquity and service and manie gay things'. Of course their living was dependent upon the fees paid for grants. We should, however, gladly know more of Shakespeare's great-grandfather or great-great-grandfather.

NATIONAL RECORDS

THE College of Heralds makes a bridge between the Court Records and the two great groups we have next to consider, both of which might be called National Records. We pass from the glorification of the Crown in its personal aspect to its justification as an instrument, firstly for establishing the reign of law in the community of the realm, and secondly for securing its efficiency between citizen and citizen. A full account of the development of National Government, as it stood in Elizabethan days, must remain outside the scope of these lectures. We must limit ourselves to noting those features of it which bear upon the personal history of Shakespeare. It is fortunate that these are comparatively few.

All the great Offices of State may be regarded as developing from the personal action of early kings, sitting in council with their supporters, their *Comites*, and turning to this one and that for advice and executive help on the matters which he understood the best. The undifferentiated council survived, in one aspect as Parliament, in another as the Privy Council, to which so much of the detail of government fell in Elizabethan days. It has since passed to the still narrower ring of the Cabinet and its subordinate Ministries. The acts of the Elizabethan Privy Council are fully preserved and are in print. They yield nothing direct upon Shakespeare, although, like the records of the City of London, much on the control of the theatres. But more specialized Departments of State had already split off from the King's Council during the Middle Ages. The *Comes*, or later the learned clerk, who helped the King with his letters, had developed into the Lord Chancellor, the head of the Chancery. The expert on finance had become the Lord High Treasurer, presiding over the Exchequer. The King's counsellors on matters of justice were organized as Judges of the High Courts of the realm. The logic was not quite complete. Some overlapping between executive and judicial functions became inevitable. So far as Records are concerned, however, we can broadly distinguish between them as on the one hand Administrative and on the other Legal. We will take the various departments in turn, and look for Shakespeare in the voluminous material which each has left. It is mostly to be found at the Public Record Office in Chancery Lane, London. A useful *Descriptive Guide* is available.

ADMINISTRATIVE RECORDS

By the fourteenth century the function of the Lord Chancellor as the writer of the King's letters had become a merely formal one. He had been replaced by the Keeper of the Privy Seal, who, in his turn, gave way during the sixteenth century to yet another, the King's Secretary, presiding over the Signet Office. Copies of the letters when written continued, however, to be preserved in the Chancery. Here they form a collection known as the Patent Rolls. They cover such matters as grants of lands by the Crown, grants of offices by the Crown, and grants for the incorporation of boroughs. Here, therefore, there should be, but is not, the grant of lands alleged by heralds to have been made to an ancestor of Shakespeare's for services to King Henry the Seventh. The grants of this reign are in a printed calendar. Those of Queen Elizabeth's time are not yet calendared, but we know that Shakespeare himself held no land direct from the Crown. Here, too, however, are patents granted to playing companies from 1603 onwards. They have been printed by the Malone Society. A second collection of Chancery records is known as the Close Rolls. It contains documents of a more private character, not all issuing from the Crown. They include copies of conveyances of lands and houses, the enrolment of which was required by an Act of Henry the Eighth's reign, especially when the conveyance was to trustees. Among them is that of Shakespeare's purchase of his Blackfriars house, the fact of which was known from this enrolment before the original deeds were discovered.

During Elizabethan days the Secretary had become in effect the chief administrative officer of the Crown, and in particular the channel of communication with ambassadors and other royal agents abroad. The post was held during 1550–72 by William Cecil, who became Lord Burghley, and during 1596–1608 by his son Robert Cecil, who became Earl of Salisbury. Each in turn was afterwards Lord High Treasurer. Secretarial documents of the Elizabethan age, letters sent and received, reports and memoranda, are very numerous, but it was not until the seventeenth century that they came to be carefully preserved as official documents. Those of the Cecil periods are much scattered. Some have found their way into the Record Office, and are calendared as *State Papers*, *Domestic*, *Foreign*, and *Irish*. Others are among the Lansdowne MSS. at the British Museum. Others again are still in the hands of the Cecil family at Hatfield House. It need not trouble us much, since the Cecils do not seem to have had occasion to concern themselves with the affairs of William Shakespeare. But in dealing with another life you might have to piece together a transaction from isolated fragments.

The Exchequer, of which the official head was the Lord Treasurer, was one of the earliest departments of State to establish itself. This was natural enough, since it dealt largely with taxation. Kings must live, and how should they live, except by taxing their subjects? The organization was an elaborate one, and threw off many sub-departments, which kept a variety of Account Rolls. These may again be studied among the documents preserved at the Record Office. We need not go into their complicated details, since only one point emerges which bears upon Shakespeare. Elizabeth was an economical sovereign, and as a rule paid her way on the proceeds of the Crown lands and the customs granted once for all by Parliament at the beginning of her reign. Towards its end, however, the cost of the Spanish war obliged her to apply for further aid. This was given in the form of Subsidies, which were taxes at the alternative rates of four shillings in the pound on the annual value of lands or two shillings and eightpence on that of personal goods. They were to be paid by instalments over a period of years. Commissioners were appointed to collect them from each county and city, with sub-commissioners for the separate hundreds or wards. These in turn nominated the actual assessors and collectors. If a collector could not, on account of absence or protest, obtain the contribution assessed on an individual, the failure was reported to the Exchequer, who noted it on the Pipe Roll, an annual survey of the Crown revenue made up for the Lord Treasurer at Michaelmas, and steps were then taken to recover the sum due through the Sheriff or other chief officer of the district in which the defaulter lived. Shakespeare was assessed during October 1596, in the parish of St. Helen's, Bishopsgate, for a payment of five shillings as the last instalment of a subsidy granted by Parliament in 1593. The collector had not obtained it by November 1597, and search for later recovery has been fruitless. Shakespeare was assessed again in the same parish for thirteen shillings and fourpence towards a new subsidy granted in 1597, and again the amount could not be collected. In this case we can trace the sequel. The arrear was entered on the Pipe Roll, and direction given, apparently not before October 1599, and not to the authorities for Bishopsgate, but to the Sheriff of Surrey, to collect it. A year later it seems to have been discovered that the debtor was not in his jurisdiction, but in that of the Bishop of Winchester, who had an independent liberty, the Clink, in Southwark; and the amount is probably included in a lump sum, for which the Bishop accounted in 1600. So hardly did early sovereigns secure their means of existence. The main interest of all this for us is in the evidence which it furnishes as to where Shakespeare lived in London. At Bishopsgate in 1596 he would have been near the playhouse known as the Theatre, where his company were then acting. By 1599 he was in the Clink, near the Globe, which had been built for them in that year. Malone, in 1796, claimed to have two documents, one showing Shakespeare in Southwark, which may mean the Clink, in 1596, the other giving presumptive evidence that he continued to reside in Southwark to 1608. Unfortunately he never published them, and the second statement may be inconsistent with evidence, to which we shall come, that in 1604 Shakespeare was lodging in Cripplegate. There is room for further investigation here. But we will now turn to the second group of National Records, which we may distinguish as Legal rather than Administrative.

LEGAL RECORDS

These are both numerous and complicated. From an early date itinerate Justices of Assize, appointed by the Crown, visited all parts of the country. We have already noted their intervention, followed by that of the Privy Council, in the matter of the Welcombe enclosure. They inquired into the proceedings of the local courts, such as the Stratford Court of Record, and on their advice a writ might be issued transferring the decision on suitable cases to superior ones at the centre of government in London. Thus by the fourteenth century had arisen the royal courts of the King's or Queen's Bench, dealing with matters both criminal and civil, in which the Crown itself was concerned, of the Common Pleas for disputed rights between citizen and citizen, and of the Exchequer for questions of taxation. These are known as the Common Law courts. Matters of equity, rather than strict law, remained under the jurisdiction of the royal Council itself, or its delegated organs in the Chancery and the Court of Requests. Some minor courts, with a more limited range, came into existence at the time of the Reformation. There was a considerable overlapping between these various organizations, largely due to legal fictions, through which officials, paid by fees, attempted to enlarge their scope. But we need not go into such matters, or consider the nature of the numerous rolls and other documents kept and still in part preserved. Shakespeare does not seem to have been litigious, and we may confine ourselves to the few known points which concern him.

Unlike Ben Jonson, when he slew an actor in a duel, Shakespeare did not bring himself within the ambit of the criminal law, although, perhaps, he was lucky to escape it. Felonies were normally tried either in the Queen's Bench or at Assizes, but in cases involving high treason by judges sitting under special commissions at Westminster Hall. Nobles, however, were entitled to a hearing by a commission of their peers. During the trial of the Earl of Essex for high treason in 1601 Shakespeare's *Richard II* was brought incidentally into question. Essex had been noted, while in disgrace at Court, as frequently witnessing performances of the play, which contained a significant deposition scene, and when it was printed in 1597 this scene, either through discretion or as the result of censorship, was rather pointedly omitted. And when the Earl was on the verge of outbreak in February 1601, his followers gave themselves heart by arranging for a special performance which they attended. This was referred to during the course of the trial, but, oddly enough, no blame seems to have been laid on the players, since, a few days later, they were called upon to present a play—not *Richard II* itself, no doubt—at Court.

There were three great High Courts with jurisdiction in matters of civil dispute. That of the Common Pleas dealt with straightforward cases, affecting property or debt or the like between subject and subject; that of the Queen's Bench with those involving an allegation of fraud or violence, which might call for punishment by the Crown; that of the Exchequer Court with those affecting the property or revenues of the Crown itself. These distinctions were not strictly observed. Court officials, paid by fees, competed for business, and by a legal fiction, such as an allegation of fraud which was not pursued, or a formal plea that, because a man had not paid you a debt, you could not pay your taxes to the Crown, a case proper, for example, to the Common Pleas was often brought in the Queen's Bench or the Exchequer. Many of the records of these courts remain in the Record Office, unpublished, and here is a field in which arduous research might still bring something fresh to light about Shakespeare.

It has indeed, quite recently, done so. In the course of an examination of the Rolls of the Queen's Bench, Professor Leslie Hotson of Haverford came upon a petition of November 1596, in which one William Wayte asked for surety of the peace against William Shakespeare, Francis

Langley, Dorothy Soer, and Anne Lee. He declared that
he acted *ob metum mortis*. This led Professor Hotson into
an elaborate study, the results of which he set out in his
Shakespeare versus Shallow of 1931. He soon unearthed
another petition in which Francis Langley, somewhat
earlier in the same November, had taken precisely the
same action against one William Gardiner, and then three
more, two in the Queen's Bench and one in the Common
Pleas, in which Gardiner had accused Langley of slander-
ing him at Croydon in Surrey on 21 and 22 May and
1 June 1596. Langley put in defences in which he claimed
to have said no more than that Gardiner had been guilty
of perjury, and this he was prepared to maintain. These
cases do not seem to have ever come to trial. Langley was
of course already known as the builder of the Swan Playhouse in Paris Garden, hard by the Clink, towards the end
of 1594, and Gardiner as one of the justices ordered by the
Privy Council to pluck down the Surrey playhouses on
28 July 1597. He had a substantial estate in Bermondsey
on the border of Southwark. An investigation of his career
by Professor Hotson was evidently desirable. It proved
to be a long 'tissue of greed, usury, fraud, cruelty and
perjury', which throws much discredit on the Elizabethan
choice of Justices of the Peace. William Wayte, his step-
son, was at once his victim and his tool. He had married
a Luce, and Professor Hotson would identify him with the
Justice Shallow of *2 Henry IV* and *The Merry Wives of
Windsor*, who might bear the dozen white luces in his coat.
But on the grounds for the quarrels with Langley and
Shakespeare, and on the part played by the two women
in November 1596, we get no further light. The first
clearly identified occupants of the Swan playhouse are
Lord Pembroke's men in February 1597. But the record
of a suit in the Court of Requests between them and

Langley a little later tells us that 'the said howse was then lately afore used to have playes in hit', and Professor Hotson conjectures that these may have been given by Shakespeare and his fellows of Lord Hunsdon's company in the autumn of 1596. Of this there may be some confirmation in Dekker's *Satiromastix*, where Tucca says, 'my name's Hamlet revenge: thou hast been at Paris Garden, hast not?' But I think that Professor Hotson goes rather beyond his evidence when he infers from the petition of November 1596 that Shakespeare was then living in Surrey, where Langley's manor of Paris Garden adjoined the Southwark Bankside, or Liberty of the Clink. It is true that Edmund Malone in 1796, on the strength of a paper which once belonged to the player Edward Alleyn, but is not now known, said that he appears to have lived in Southwark, near the Bear Garden, in 1596. He adds, from another lost document then in his possession, that the residence in Southwark lasted to 1608. But we know, from a source to which we shall come, that in 1604 Shakespeare was lodging in Cripplegate. No doubt the petition of November 1596 shows him in relations with Langley at the Swan, but if he was acting there it may have been only at the beginning or end of a tour by Lord Hunsdon's men, which took them farther afield, since about 1 August 1596 they gave a performance at Faversham in Kent. Moreover, we have from Exchequer Records some facts as to taxes due from him. In October 1596 he was assessed in St. Helen's, Bishopsgate, for a sum of 5*s*. due towards a subsidy, in respect of property worth £5. It was payable in February 1597. But in the following November the collectors reported that they could not obtain it, and in fact it does not seem to have been recovered by 1613–14. That, taken alone, would not have been inconsistent with a removal from Bishopsgate. But another subsidy became payable in 1599, and for his contribution to that Shakespeare was again assessed in St. Helen's. Again it was not forthcoming there when it became due in the winter of 1598–9. Investigation by the Exchequer authorities seems to have traced Shakespeare to Surrey by October 1599, and more precisely to the Bishop of Winchester's Liberty of the Clink by 6 October 1600. My impression is that he moved to Southwark when the Globe was built there during 1599.

It is from the Queen's Bench also that comes the record of a suit between John Shakespeare and his nephew John Lambert about an affair of property with which William seems to have been concerned. It had become the King's Bench by 1615, when there was another between his fellow-actor John Heminges and the representative of a second, Thomasina Ostler, concerning the rights to shares in the Globe and Blackfriars Theatres. Shakespeare was not a party to this, but a pleading recites the transactions by which he and others became entitled to their interests in those houses.

The records of the Common Pleas, apart from the abortive slander case between Gardiner and Langley already referred to, only concern us as containing those curious fictitious suits for the further assurance of conveyances of lands and houses, by way of 'fines', which we came across in considering Tenurial Records. And from the Exchequer Court we only get the facts as to the collection of Shakespeare's contributions to subsidies.

But the activity of these three great courts of law did not exhaust the possibilities of doing justice at head-quarters between subjects of the Crown. Their function was limited to administering the Common Law of the realm, and the additions made to it by Parliamentary statutes. There remained an inherent right in the Crown to do justice between subjects in matters not so covered. And so, side by side with Courts of Common Law, had grown up others, which may be distinguished as Courts of Equity.

The most important of these was the Court of Chancery, presided over by the Lord Chancellor, whose functions in this respect had grown in importance, while those as the channel for the king's letters had become little more than formal. Two Chancery suits concern Shakespeare. One arose out of his sublease of tithes at Stratford, the other out of his purchase of a house in Blackfriars. But both of these we have already considered under the heading of Tenurial Records.

A minor Court of Equity was that of Requests. This had been established by Cardinal Wolsey in the time of Henry VIII, to provide a remedy for the wrongs of poor suitors, who could not afford the high fees charged in Chancery actions. It came, however, also to be used for disputes among members of the royal Household, and therefore for those of the King's players, who ranked among these. Such a suit was that of John Witter *versus* John Heminge and Henry Condell in 1619. This was after Shakespeare's death, but it concerned the Globe Theatre, and incidentally a recital shows the nature and origin of Shakespeare's financial interest therein. In an earlier suit in this court Shakespeare himself appears. During 1612 he was called upon as a witness in the case of Belott *versus* Mountjoy. Christopher Mountjoy was a Huguenot refugee, by occupation a tiremaker, living in Silver Street, Cripplegate. Stephen Belott, also a Huguenot, had married his daughter Mary, as far back as 1604, and now claimed that his father-in-law had failed to hand over her promised portion. It was given in evidence that Shakespeare was lodging at Mountjoy's house, when the wedding took place, and had been a go-between in bringing it about. He was called upon to bear witness as to what he knew of the circumstances. We have his signed deposition to the effect that he could not remember the precise amount of the portion promised. Unfortunately the body of the document is not in his hand, but we get one more signature to add to those in the will and the Blackfriars deed. Do we also learn that he was already of failing memory in 1612, or was he merely unwilling to take a side between the parties? He says that he had known them both since about 1602. Incidentally it appears from the case that neither of them, in 1612, bore a good character.

A suit of 1638 in the Requests has an incidental reference to Shakespeare's Henley Street property at Stratford in 1609.

PERSONAL RECORDS

THE Records so far considered are primarily those of institutions. Of course there is a personal element in them; that is their interest for us. We turn now to others which are of a more intimately personal character. All biographers welcome an autobiography, or a diary, or a contemporary narrative, such as James Boswell wrote for Samuel Johnson. Failing these, or supplementing them, they look for letters, which come nearer to the inner man than formal documents. Coleridge's life, for example, can almost be written from his letters alone. Letters normally remain in personal custody, although not that of the writer. He may keep drafts or copies in a letter-book, but this is not very usual, unless the letters are of an official or business character. There may also be memoranda or account books, if the subject of the biography was methodical enough to preserve them. Poets are not, as a rule. There are those, of course, who will tell you that Shakespeare was primarily a business man, and only a poet by accident. There is no limit to the odd things people will say about Shakespeare.

Shakespeare left no autobiography or diary. Whether any autobiographical elements can be found in the *Sonnets*, or even in the plays, is a question of literary criticism, and we will not discuss it, if at all, under the head of Records. Nor had he a Boswell. Such brief contemporary allusions as exist were not meant for the information of posterity. Nor have we any letters from him except the two formal dedications of his poems to the Earl of Southampton. We have one letter addressed to him, a request in 1598 for a loan by Richard Quiney, a Stratford citizen who visited London in 1598, and whose son Thomas later married the poet's daughter Judith. It may never have reached him, since it was found, much folded up, in a bundle of correspondence belonging to the Quiney family. Possibly Richard met Shakespeare after writing it, and had no need to send it. Some other letters of the Quiney family suggest a desire to persuade Shakespeare to make an investment in Stratford, as he did in fact at a later date.

It is probable that papers belonging to Shakespeare were in existence at the time of his death. They are most likely to have been at New Place, but some may have been at his Blackfriars house. Both of these passed to his daughter Susanna, who in 1607 had married John Hall. The Blackfriars house was sold at a date not later than 1647 to one Edward Bagley, apparently a kinsman, in some unknown degree, of the Halls, from whom it passed in 1667 to Sir Heneage Fetherston. Susanna Hall died in 1649, leaving New Place to her daughter Elizabeth, who married Thomas Nash in 1627, and after his death in 1647 took a second husband in John, who later became Sir John, Bernard. She died in 1670 and he in 1674. There were no children by either marriage. New Place also passed to Edward Bagley, who sold it in 1675 to Sir Edward Walker. Through a marriage with Walker's daughter Barbara it became the property of the Clopton family, and was later sold to the Reverend Francis Gastrell, who pulled it down in 1759.

Any papers left by Shakespeare would have passed to John Hall and Susanna under a residual bequest of 'goodes, chattels, leases, plate, jewels, and housholde stufe' in his will. A nuncupative one of Hall in 1635 has the following entry.

Item Concerning my Study of Bookes I leave them (sayde hee) to yow my sonn Nash to dispose of them as yow see good. As for my Manuscriptes I would haue giuen them to Mr Boles if hee had been here. But forasmuch as hee is not heere present, yow may son Nash burne them or doe with them what yow please.

He is thinking of his own papers rather than Shakespeare's. Boles was probably Joseph Bowles, a fellow physician of Hall's at Stratford. In 1637 one Baldwin Brooks brought an action against Susanna Hall and Thomas Nash for an alleged debt due to him from John Hall, and Susanna deposed that since her husband's death Brooks had sent bailiffs into her house, and added,

The said Bayliffes did then and there breake open the Doores and studdy of the said howse and Rashlye seize vppon and take Divers bookes boxes Deskes moneys bonds bills and other goods of greate value.

That is all we learn, which may possibly cover papers at New Place, for nearly half a century. If there were any of Shakespeare's, they may have either remained there or passed after Lady Bernard's death in 1670 to her husband's house at Abington in Northants. When he too died in 1674 he left a study of books, and some 'old goods and lumber at Stratford'.

After another half-century gossip begins. In 1729 one John Roberts wrote:

How much is it to be lamented, that Two large Chests full of this Great Man's loose Papers and Manuscripts, in the Hands of an ignorant Baker of Warwick (who married one of the Descendants from Shakespeare) were carelessly Scatter'd and thrown about, as Garret Lumber and Litter, to the particular Knowledge of the late Sir William Bishop, till they were all consum'd in the generall Fire and Destruction of that Town.

There was such a fire in 1694, but we do not know that any descendant of Shakespeare ever lived at Warwick. Sir William Bishop, who died in 1700, was of Bridgetown, on the edge of Stratford. John Jordan in 1780 has a similar story, but adds that the papers were burnt in a conflagration at Stratford, while they were in Bishop's hands. He knew a tradition that they were once in the hands of a baker, a quite imaginary descendant of the poet. There had not, he says, been a conflagration at Stratford since 1614. One Charles Macklin says he was told in 1742 by Sir Hugh Clopton, who then owned New Place, that Lady Bernard had carried with her from Stratford many of her grandfather's papers. It is likely enough, but in 1748 Macklin published some anecdotes on Shakespeare which were certainly fabrications. Samuel Ireland, who visited Stratford in 1794, was told that, on the destruction of New Place in 1759, papers from it were removed to the chief house of the Clopton family a mile from Stratford. He tried for Shakespeare manuscripts there, but without success. He was accompanied by his son William Henry Ireland, who had already started upon his career as a Shakespearian forger, and in 1796 and 1805 declared that one Williams, a gentleman-farmer who then occupied that house, had said to him:

By God, I wish you had arrived a little sooner! why, it isn't a fortnight since I destroyed several baskets-full of letters and papers, in order to clear a small chamber for some young partridges which I wish to bring up alive: and as to Shakespeare, why there were many bundles with his name wrote upon them. Why it was in this very fire-place I made a roaring bonfire of them.

Tradition is here merging in burlesque. Samuel also claimed in 1805 to have seen in public prints that two letters from Shakespeare, written to Thomas Sackville, Earl of Dorset, had been discovered at Knole in Kent. But neither the letters nor the public prints are forthcoming. In 1818 Sir Richard Phillips stated, on the authority of Mary Hornby, then caretaker of the Henley Street houses, that a letter from Shakespeare to his wife had been recovered some years before from a very small deep cupboard in a dark corner of the room in which the poet was born. She used to show it to visitors, but a party to whom it was lent went off without returning it. Finally, as late as 1851 it was stated by Robert Bigsby in his *Old Places Revisited* that letters by or about Shakespeare had been found among the papers of a Colonel William Gardiner, of Thurgarton, Notts., a descendant of the Bernard family, who died in 1806. I do not know whether this has ever been verified, but obviously the Bernard family would be a very natural channel of transmission.

But, if letters fail, what then is left to us of Shakespeare's Hand? There are six legal signatures, some rather abbreviated. Three are in the will, two in the Blackfriars conveyance and mortgage, one in the Belott *versus* Mountjoy suit. There are two more in printed books. Of these one, probably genuine, is in the British Museum copy of John Florio's translation (1603) of Montaigne's *Essayes*, the other, more doubtful, in the Bodleian copy of Ovid's

Metamorphoses (1502). There are over a hundred others, all forgeries, many of them due to the incorrigible W. H. Ireland. John Heminge and Henry Condell, in their preface to the First Folio of the Plays, tell us of the writer:

> His mind and hand went together: and what he thought, he vttered with that easinesse, that wee haue scarce receiued from him a blot in his papers.

Early manuscripts of two plays were once at Warwick Castle, and are now, I believe, in the Folger Collection at Washington, but they are not Shakespeare's autographs. On the other hand, recent criticism tends to ascribe to him the script of three pages in a play of *Sir Thomas More*, which appears to have been originally written by Anthony Munday about 1593 and later expanded by more than one contributor. There is no contemporary print of it. The argument for Shakespeare's participation is based partly on the rather slight evidence provided by his undisputed signatures, but also upon the presence of spellings which might explain misprints in the Quartos and Folio of his undoubted plays, and upon characteristic motives common to *Sir Thomas More* and to those. I think that it is probably sound.

Some recent speculations probably do not help us, although I do not feel sure how far they have received competent examination. In 1936 an anonymous writer in the *Observer* (9 Feb.) described a copy of the second edition of Holinshed's *Chronicles* (1587), then in the hands of the Comtesse Clara Longworth de Chambrun at Paris, and declared that it contained markings and annotations in Shakespeare's hand. This opinion was supported by the Comtesse herself in her *Shakespeare Rediscovered* (1937). In 1940 an anonymous correspondent of *The Times* (29 Aug.) argued for the authenticity of a number of annotations in a copy of Edward Hall's *Chronicles* (1550). He relied not on the handwriting, although he found a certain similarity to the accepted signatures, but on the use of rare words in a Shakespearian sense, on parallelisms of language, on the fact that everything so noted was used in the chronicle plays, and on a belief that they were 'the sort of notes which would only be made by a reader who was jotting things down with a view to constructing a play'. Mr. Alan Keen, the discoverer of the notes, wrote later that they dealt chiefly with the reigns of Richard II, Henry IV, and Henry V, but it was pointed out by Mr. R. F. W. Fletcher that Shakespeare's *Henry V* was certainly based not upon Hall, but upon Holinshed. It must be obvious that bare and sometimes contracted signatures are a poor basis on which to identify continuous script.

One other record is of an unusual type. In 1613 the steward of Francis Manners, Earl of Rutland, paid

To Mr Shakspeare in gold about my Lorde's impreso xliiijs; to Richard Burbage for paynting and makying yt, in gold xliiijs, —iiij li viiij s.

An *impresa* was a painted shield of paper, with emblems and mottoes. This one was for use at an Accession Day tilt. Presumably Shakespeare contributed the mottoes.

Portraits, of course, must be classed as personal records, but of these again few exist on which we can rely with any confidence. The half-length figure in the monument at Stratford Church is ascribed to Gerard Janssen, of an emigrant family from Amsterdam. The engraving in the Folio of 1623 is by Martin Droeshout, of a Flemish family long settled in London. Jonson praises it in appended verses, as one

> Wherein the Grauer had a strife
> with Nature, to out-doo the life.

Of the others two have some interest. The so-called 'Flower' portrait in the Shakespeare memorial at Stratford has an unverifiable history of derivation from a descendant of Shakespeare. It bears the date 1609, but was not improbably based on the Folio engraving. The Chandos portrait in the National Portrait Gallery is ascribed to the brush of the actor Richard Burbage, but does not resemble the Janssen figure or the engraving, and was probably not taken from life. With the rest we need not concern ourselves.

We have now been, very summarily, through the main groups of documentary Records available for Shakespeare's life. Let me recapitulate them. They are Tenurial, Ecclesiastical, Municipal, Occupational, Court, National, and Personal. Roughly speaking, you have to consider the same possible kinds of record for any other life analogous to that of Shakespeare. Unless you get more intimate personal records, such as an autobiography or letters, a survey must remain rather colourless, limited to external transactions, apt to be formal. There will, of course, be individual variations. With a literary man, you may need to examine university records; with a lawyer, those of the Inns of Court; with a tradesman, those of commercial guilds. With a man, such as Sir Walter Raleigh, who took part in public affairs, the papers of the Privy Council and the Secretary of State will be important.

As to Shakespeare himself, I will not say that the door is closed. There is that big hiatus of 1584–92. What was he doing in it? I have made one guess. Family papers have not all been ransacked. Those of Edward Bagley, to whom Shakespeare's Blackfriars house and New Place passed, might turn up. The archives of the Bernard family might yield something. There are many unexplored documents in the records of the Law Courts, especially the Chancery, and in those of the City of London at the Guildhall. Systematic and arduous research would be involved. Perhaps a lucky accident is more likely to bear fruit.

Records, in the widest sense, do not exhaust the material available for the study of Shakespeare's personal life. We have still to consider, with discretion, (*a*) Contemporary allusions to him by other writers, (*b*) Traditions emerging after his death, and (*c*) Inferences drawn from his non-dramatic writings, and in particular from his *Sonnets*.

CONTEMPORARY ALLUSIONS

THERE are of course many references to Shakespeare's theatrical career in the writings of contemporaries. Most of them will be found in *The Shakspere Allusion-Book*, of which the latest edition is that by J. Munro (1932). We will continue to limit ourselves, as far as possible, for the purposes of these lectures, to those which are not merely literary, but throw some light, often very faint, on the poet's personality as a man. Some of them, it must be added, are very doubtful. Thus Edmund Spenser, in his *The Teares of the Muses* (1591), writing on the decadence of the comic stage, tells us:

> And he the man, whom Nature selfe had made
> To mock her selfe, and Truth to imitate,
> With kindly counter vnder Mimick shade,
> Our pleasant *Willy*, ah is dead of late:
> With whom all ioy and iolly merriment
> Is also deaded, and in dolour drent.

And he adds:

> But that same gentle Spirit, from whose pen
> Large streames of honnie and sweete Nectar flowe,
> Scorning the boldnes of such base-borne men,
> Which dare their follies forth so rashlie throwe;

> Doth rather choose to sit in idle Cell,
> Than so himself to mockery to sell.

It is very difficult, in view of anything we know of Shakespeare's beginnings, to suppose that he could have been written on in such terms as early as 1591. A little more plausible is another Spenserian passage in *Colin Clout's Come Home Againe*, since this, although also extant in some form by 1591, may have been revised before it was published in 1595.

> And there though last not least is *Aetion*,
> A gentler shepheard may no where be found:
> Whose *Muse* full of high thoughts inuention,
> Doth like himselfe Heroically sound.

Certainly Shakespeare's name has a heroic ring about it. An alternative candidate is Michael Drayton. But throughout we must beware of seeing everything through Shakespeare spectacles. There is a lack of perspective in this. It is unreasonable to suppose that Shakespeare was from the beginning what he came to be, and is still to us, or that he was the centre of all the literary feuds which have left obscure traces in Elizabethan writings.

One other literary reference shall be quoted, not because there is anything very personal, in the narrower sense, about it, but because the poem in which it occurs has only been recently printed in its full form. It was written by Francis Beaumont to Ben Jonson, probably about 1615, and in it he says:

> heere I would let slippe
> (If I had any in mee) schollershippe,
> And from all Learninge keepe these lines as cleere
> As Shakespeares best are, which our heires shall heare
> Preachers apte to their auditors to showe
> How farr sometimes a mortall man may goe
> By the dimme light of Nature.

It is a graceful epilogue to Shakespeare's literary life, then approaching its close.

But we are concerned with the *personalia*. There are not many which are recorded for us by writers who can reasonably be called contemporary. The first of these is Robert Greene, himself a playwright, who in his *Groats-worth of Wit* (1592) warns his fellows against the players, who are likely to forsake them.

Yes trust them not: for there is an vpstart Crow, beautified with our feathers, that with his *Tygers hart wrapt in a Players hyde*, supposes he is as well able to bombast out a blanke verse as the best of you: and beeing an absolute Iohannes fac totum, is in his owne conceit the onely Shake-scene in a countrey.

Greene was evidently parodying *3 Henry VI*, i. iv. 137:

O tiger's heart wrapt in a woman's hide!

His book was referred to by Henry Chettle in the Epistle to his *Kind-Hart's Dreame* (1592), where he notes that it was offensively taken by one or two playwrights. And of one of those he says that he regrets Greene's criticism.

Because my selfe have seene his demeanor no lesse ciuill than he exelent in the qualitie he professes: Besides, diuers of worship haue reported his uprightness of dealing, which argues his honesty, and his facetious grace in writting, that aprooues his Art.

It is possible that Chettle may be here referring to Shakespeare. He certainly is later in his *England's Mourning Garment* (1603) when he writes:

Nor doth the siluer tonged *Melicert*
Drop from his honied muse one sable teare
To mourne her death that graced his desert,
And to his laies opend her Royal eare.
        Shepheard, remember our *Elizabeth*,
        And sing her Rape, done by that *Tarquin*, Death.

But Shakespeare was not drawn.

Francis Meres in his *Palladis Tamia* (1598), amid much praise of Shakespeare, notes 'his sugred Sonnets among his priuate friends'. The anonymous writer of Part II of *The Returne from Parnassus* (1601?) makes the actor William Kempe say of university playwrights:

Why heres our fellow Shakespeare puts them all downe, I and Ben Jonson too. O that Ben Jonson is a pestilent fellow, he brought up Horace giuing the Poets a pill, but our fellow Shakespeare hath giuen him a purge that made him beray his credit.

We do not know what play, if the purge was in a play, is referred to. John Manningham in his *Diary* for 1602 has a story of a woman who so much admired Richard Burbage in the part of Richard III that she made an appointment with him for a love-affair. Shakespeare overheard and took his place, sending him a message that William the Conqueror came before Richard III. But this is an adaptation of an old motive, traceable in late Greek and in French and Italian literature, long before Manningham's day. Thomas Heywood, in his *An Apology for Actors* (1612) says that two of his own poems had been printed as Shakespeare's in the *Passionate Pilgrim*, and 'the author I know much offended with M. Jaggard that (altogether unknown to him) presumed to make so bold with his name'.

The First Folio Edition of Shakespeare's plays appeared, some seven years after his death, in 1623. It contains, among other prefatory matter, some personal references, which may be regarded as contemporary, both by Ben Jonson and by the poet's fellow actors John Heminge and Henry Condell. In one set of verses Jonson writes of him as 'gentle Shakespeare', in another as 'my beloued' and as 'Sweet Swan of Auon'. Heminge and Condell dedicate the book to William, Earl of Pembroke, the Lord Chamberlain, and Philip, Earl of Montgomery, a Gentleman of the Bedchamber, who have, they say of the plays, 'profequuted both them and their Authour liuing, with so much fauour'. In a further preface to the readers they add of Shakespeare himself:

His mind and hand went together: and what he thought, he vttered with that eafineffe, that wee haue fcarfe receiued from him a blot in his papers.

One other probable contemporary allusion of as early a date as 1594, in Henry Willoughby's *Avisa*, has been the subject of controversy, and will be best discussed in connexion with the *Sonnets*. We will turn now to the topic of Traditions.

TRADITIONS

Traditions as to Shakespeare's personality begin to emerge soon after his death and continue to be frequent for well over a century and a half later. Stratford became a place of pilgrimage, and any information furnished by its inn-keepers or their servants no doubt met with its due reward. Some local gentlemen, however, such as Sir William Bishop, also made their contribution. An independent stream of gossip came from the green rooms of the London theatres. The results have reached us through many writers. The fullest recorder is John Aubrey (1681). Others are Richard James (c. 1625), Lieutenant Hammond (1634), Sir Nicholas L'Estrange (c. 1629–35), Thomas Fuller (1643–61), Thomas Plume (c. 1657), John Ward (1661–3), David Lloyd (1665), John Dryden (1672), Robert Dobyns (1673), Edward Ravenscroft (1678), Richard Davies (1688–1708), Joshua Barnes (c. 1690), Anthony Wood (1692), Mr. Dowdall (1693), Charles Gildon (1694–1700), James

Wright (1699), John Dennis (1702–4), John Downes
(1708), Thomas Hearne (1709), Lewis Theobald (1727),
Joseph Spence (1728–43), Francis Peck (1740), Charles
Macklin (1742), William Oldys (c. 1743–61), John Jordan
(1770–90, a forger), Edward Capell (1780), S. Cooper
(1788), Sir Walter Scott (1828), S. W. Fullom (1862). A
few other contributors are anonymous. Some of the stories
found their way into the first literary edition of Shakespeare's plays by Nicholas Rowe (1709), who had material
from the actor Thomas Betterton (1635–1710). For a more
critical attitude we have to await the researches of Edmund
Malone, which began in 1773, and took their final form
in an edition of the plays issued after his death by James
Boswell in 1821 and now known as the *Third Variorum
Shakespeare*. Malone is very critical of Rowe, in whose
Life, he said, not more than eleven facts were mentioned,
of which eight would be found to be false. But even
Malone's learning did not wholly stop the growth of what
may be called the Shakespeare *Mythos*. As late as 1879
emerged a story, said to be found in the diary of one
Dr. Frank Chambers, dated in 1794 and preserved in the
British Museum, that Horace Walpole had offered £300
for Shakespeare's skull, that the doctor had hired three
local ruffians to dig it up, that Walpole had refused to
take it, and that it was buried again in the church of
Studley in Warwickshire, where was a manor-house called
Gorcott Hall, long occupied by a Chambers family. I
hasten to add that, although my own family came from
Warwickshire and had a common ancestry with that of
Gorcott, the descents were distinct from the sixteenth century onwards. I cannot find a Frank Chambers in the
Gorcott pedigree, but the Christian names of some
children of a Thomas, who died in 1802, are missing.

But we will return to the seventeenth- and eighteenth-century traditions, and classify them as far as possible by their origin and subject-matter. It will rarely be necessary to estimate their validity in detail. Any comments I make shall be brief.

EARLY LIFE AT STRATFORD

Of this we are told little. Shakespeare's father (Aubrey) or early master (Dowdall) was a butcher. As a boy he exercised his father's trade. When he killed a calf, he would do it in a high style, and make a speech (Aubrey). He was bred at a free school (Rowe). He was in his younger years a schoolmaster in the county (Aubrey).

The most widespread story, although it emerges late, is that of his *Hegira* from Stratford. We will give it rather full treatment, as a good example of the divergent forms which tradition sometimes takes. According to Davies (1688–1708), Shakespeare was 'much given to all unluckiness in stealing venison and rabbits, particularly from Sir . . . Lucy, who had him oft whipped and sometimes imprisoned and at last made him fly his native county to his great advancement, but his revenge was so great that he is his Justice Clodpate, and calls him a great man and that in allusion to his name bore three louses rampant for his arms'. The knight intended was clearly Sir Thomas Lucy, of Charlecote and Fulbrook, near Stratford, whose arms were 'Gules, semée of cross-crosslets Or, three luces haurient Argent'. Luces are pikes. There is no Justice Clodpate in Shakespeare's plays. A 'clodpate' is a 'blockhead'. The allusion is to *Merry Wives of Windsor*, I. i, where Justice Shallow threatens to bring Sir John Falstaff into the Star Chamber, and is backed by his cousin Slender, who describes him as entitled to bear the 'dozen white luces' in his coat. Sir Hugh Evans, who stands by, calls them 'white louses'. Falstaff enters, and Shallow upbraids him. 'Knight, you have beaten my men, kill'd my deer, and broke open my lodge.' The next version is by Rowe (1709), perhaps derived from the actor Thomas Betterton, who is said to have visited Warwickshire in 1708. Shakespeare 'had, by a misfortune common enough to young fellows fallen into ill company; and amongst them, some that made a frequent practice of deer-stealing, engag'd him with them more than once in robbing a park that belong'd to Sir Thomas Lucy of Charlecot, near Stratford. For this he was prosecuted by that gentleman, as he thought, somewhat too severely; and in order to revenge that ill usage, he made a ballad upon him. And tho' this, probably the first essay of his poetry, be lost, yet it is said to have been so very bitter, that it redoubled the prosecution against him to that degree, that he was oblig'd to leave his business and family in Warwickshire, for some time, and shelter himself in London.' Malone cites from a manuscript History of the Stage (1727–30), probably written by William Chetwood, a theatrical prompter, and full of forgeries and falsehoods, a statement that Joshua Barnes, a Cambridge professor, visiting Stratford some forty years earlier, heard an old woman singing two stanzas of Shakespeare's ballad, and gave her two guineas out of respect for the poet's genius. They are quoted, in quatrains, and represent Lucy not only as covetous about his deer, but also as a cuckold. Oldys (c. 1743–61) also claims to have heard a stanza of the 'bitter ballad' from a gentleman who visited Stratford fifty years before. But his version, which plays on the jingle of 'lowsie Lucy', is quite different from that given by Chetwood. Oldys (c. 1750) says that the ballad was affixed to Lucy's park-gates, and notes the use of its jingle in the Merry Wives. Oldys also repeats Rowe's account of Shakespeare's misdemeanour, as derived from Betterton. A writer in the Biographia

Britannica (1763) tells us that 'This ballad was not the only shaft which he let fly against his persecutor, whose anger drove him to the extreme end of ruin, where he was forced to a very low degree of drudgery for a support;—how long the knight continued inexorable is not known; but it is certain that Shakespeare owed his release at last to the Queen's kindness.' Capell (1780) obtained 'many years ago' the same stanza of the ballad as that given by Oldys, with an elaborate pedigree of it by the donor, one Mr. Wilkes. According to this, Thomas Jones of Tardebigge, near Stratford, who died over ninety years old in 1703, had heard from old people in the town of the raid on Lucy's park, with the addition that Shakespeare's ballad 'was stuck upon the park gate, which exasperated the knight to apply to a lawyer at Warwick to proceed against him'. Jones gave the stanza to one Thomas Wilkes, and he to his son, from whom it passed to Capell. John Jordan (*c.* 1790), a wheelwright of Tiddington near Stratford, shifts the scene of Shakespeare's exploit from Charlecote to Fulbrook, and claimed to give a complete text of the 'satirical song' in the 'lousie Lucy' version, 'which inflamed Sir Thomas to the utmost pitch, and he renewed the prosecution with the utmost vigour'. Malone thought that this was a forgery. Actually there was no 'park', in the technical sense, at either Charlecote or Fulbrook by the supposed date, but there may have been a few deer in the demesnes. When he told his story again to Samuel Ireland in 1794, Jordan pointed to a farm-house called Daisy Hill, once the keeper's lodge, as the place at which Shakespeare was confined. The legend becomes more precise as it grows older. Cooper (1788) gave the locality as Charlecote, but put it erroneously near Ingon, which is a good way from either Charlecote or Fulbrook. Phillips (1818) added the detail that the deer was stolen to celebrate

Shakespeare's wedding day. Scott (1828) was told at Charlecote that the buck was taken from a park of Lucy's, at some distance, and hidden in a barn. He probably means Fulbrook. Fullom (1862) learnt from Mrs. Lucy that there was proof of the story in a manuscript pedigree, compiled ninety years before, by one Ward, from records of the family. The ballad was nailed on the Charlecote park-gates. It was the Earl of Leicester, after a quarrel with Lucy, who remembered Justice Shallow, and persuaded Shakespeare to bring Lucy again on the stage. Shallow is of course in *2 Henry IV*, as well as in *The Merry Wives*, but there is nothing about the deer-stealing there. This Ward of about 1772 is of course not the John Ward who retailed other Shakespearean gossip in 1661–3.

I do not feel able to accept the theory of Professor Leslie Hotson, who identifies Shallow, not with Lucy, but with the William Gardiner of Bermondsey, with whom, as we have seen, Shakespeare had a lawsuit in 1596, although Gardiner too, by marriage with a Luce, was able to impale luces in his coat. But, as Hotson points out, this would oblige us to put *The Merry Wives* before Gardiner's death on 26 November 1597, since a scoff at him would have little point later. It is true that some features of the play would make it very suitable for performance at a Garter feast, and Hotson notes a splendid one on 23 April 1597. But if it was then produced, it would surely have been included in the very full list of Shakespeare's plays given by Francis Meres in his *Palladis Tamia* of 1598. I think Professor Hotson skates rather too lightly round this obstacle. And the whole tradition, to which the deer-stealing and the louses belong, is clearly a Stratford and not a London one.

The Man of the Theatre

(1) *Shakespeare and Jonson*. Tradition has tended to dwell
upon the personal relations between the two great outstanding dramatists of Elizabethan days. No explanation
has ever been found of David Lloyd's reference in 1665 to
Fulke Greville, Lord Brooke, as 'desiring to be known to
posterity as Shakespear's and Ben Jonson's Master'. It
is of course possible that the Grevilles may have maintained domestic players at Beauchamp Court. According
to Rowe, Shakespeare introduced Jonson to the stage.
Gossip clung around their intercourse in taverns. Fuller
describes it, 'many were the *wit-combates* betwixt him and
Ben Johnson, which two I behold like a *Spanish great Gallion*
and an *English man of War*; Master *Johnson* (like the former)
was built far higher in Learning; *Solid* but *Slow* in his
performances. *Shake-spear*, with the *English-man of War*,
lesser in *bulk*, but lighter in *sailing*, could turn with all
tides, back about and take advantage of all winds, by the
quickness of his Wit and Invention.' Of the wit we have
some examples. Shakespeare was godfather to one of
Jonson's sons (L'Estrange). After a deep study he told
Jonson he had resolved on a gift. 'I pry'the what, sayes
he? I faith *Ben*: I'le e'en giue him a douzen good Lattin
⟨latten⟩ Spoones, and thou shalt translate them.' The
same story recurs (Plume) with the relationship inverted.
Jonson began an epitaph for himself, 'Here lies Ben Johnson that was once one', and Shakespeare finished it, 'who
while hee liu'de was a sloe thinge, and now being dead
is Nothinge' (Anon., Plume). At a tavern where lords were
present, a toast was called for. Either Jonson or Shakespeare named a lord's wife that sat by. Asked why he
named her, 'Why not, replied the poet, she has the quali-
fications of a toast, being both brown and dry' (Anon.).

Jonson had a critical mind, and did not always spare Shakespeare. In his *Timber* (1623–37), he wrote, 'I *remember*, the Players have often mentioned it as an honour to *Shakespeare*, that in his writing (whatsoever he penn'd) hee never blotted out line. My answer hath beene, would he had blotted a thousand. Which they thought a malevolent speech. I had not told posterity this, but for their ignorance, who choose that circumstance to commend their friend by, wherein he most faulted. And to justifie mine own candor (for I lov'd the man, and doe honour his memory, on this Side Idolatry, as much as any.) Hee was (indeed) honest, and of an open, and free nature: had an excellent *Phantasie*; brave notions, and gentle expressions: wherein hee flow'd with that facility, that sometime it was necessary he should be stop'd: *Sufflaminandus erat*; as *Augustus* said of *Haterius*. His wit was in his own power; would the rule of it had beene so too. Many times he fell into those things, could not escape laughter: as when hee said in the person of *Caesar*, one speaking to him; *Caesar thou dost me wrong*. Hee replyed: *Caesar did never wrong, but with just cause* and such like: which were ridiculous. But he redeemed his vices, with his vertues. There was ever more in him to be praysed, than to be pardoned.' John Hales of Eton was once present at a discussion at which Sir John Suckling had defended Shakespeare against Jonson, and cut in. 'Mr. *Hales*, who had sat still for some time, hearing *Ben* frequently reproaching him with the want of Learning, and Ignorance of the Antients, told him at last, that if Mr. *Shakespear* had not read the Antients, he had likewise not stollen any thing from 'em; (a Fault the other made no Conscience of) and that if he would produce any one Topick finely treated by any of them, he would undertake to shew something upon the same Subject at least as well written by Shakespear.' Two slighter references may be added. 'In reading some bombast speeches of *Macbeth*, which are not to be understood, Ben Johnson used to say that it was horrour' (Dryden). 'One told Ben Johnson—Shakespear never studied for any thing he wrott. J. said, the more to blame He' (Plume). According to Joseph Spence (1728–43), 'It was a general opinion, that Ben Jonson and Shakspeare lived in enmity against one another. Betterton has assured one often, that there was nothing in it: and that such a supposition was founded only on the two parties, which in their lifetime listed under one, and endeavoured to lessen the character of the other mutually.' Jonson had, of course, a critical mind, but I see nothing here to qualify the general admiration for Shakespeare, which he expresses in the *First Folio*.

(2) *Shakespeare's Quality.* 'He was a handsome well shap't man: very good company, and of a readie and pleasant smooth Witt.' 'He was not a company keeper, wouldnt be debauched, and if invited to, writ he was in paine' (Aubrey). 'He was in himself a good-natur'd Man, of great sweetness in his Manners, and a most agreeable Companion' (Rowe). He 'was a natural wit, without any art at all' (Ward).

(3) *His Beginnings.* 'He was at first in a very mean rank' (Rowe). 'He picked up a little money by taking care of the gentlemen's horses who came to the play; he became eminent even in that profession, and was taken notice of for his diligence and skill in it; he had soon more business than he himself could manage, and at last hired boys under him, who were known by the name of Shakespear's boys: Some of the players accidentally conversing with him, found him so acute, and master of so fine a conversation, that struck therewith, they recommended him to the house' (Shiels, Johnson, Phillips). 'There is a stage tradition that his first office in the theatre was that of *Call-boy*, or prompter's attendant' (Malone).

(4) *His Acting*. 'He did act exceedingly well' (Aubrey). 'He was a much better Poet, than Player' (Wright). 'He was not an extraordinary Actor.' 'The top of his Performance was the Ghost in his own *Hamlet*' (Rowe). A younger brother, who lived to the Restoration, could only tell the players of 'having once seen him act a part in one of his own comedies, wherein being to personate a decrepit old man, he wore a long beard, and appeared so weak and drooping and unable to walk, that he was forced to be supported and carried by another person to a table, at which he was seated among some company, who were eating, and one of them sang a song' (Oldys). Capell had a similar story from Stratford. The part was that of Adam in *As You Like It*. In fact no brother of Shakespeare's lived to the Restoration. Capell adds that for such parts 'he might also be peculiarly fitted by an accidental lameness, which,—as he himself tells us twice in his *Sonnets*—befell him in some part of life'. Capell has of course misinterpreted the *Sonnets*, which do not refer to a physical lameness. Shakespeare trained John Lowin and Joseph Taylor (Downes). But Taylor only began acting in 1619.

(5) *His Vogue at Court*. By the *Merry Wives* he 'pleas'd one of the greatest Queens that ever was in the world. This Comedy was written at her Command, and by her direction, and she was so eager to see it Acted, that she commanded it to be finished in fourteen days' (Dennis). Elizabeth 'without doubt gave him many gracious Marks of her Favour. She was so well pleased with that admirable Character of *Falstaff* in the two Parts of *Henry* the Fourth, that she commanded him to continue it for one Play more, and to shew him in Love' (Rowe). While he acted a king on the stage, he would not throw off his character to notice her. As he was about to make his exit

she stepped before him, and dropped her glove on the
stage. Shakespeare picked it up, with the words:

> And though now bent on this high embassy,
> Yet *stoop* we to take up our *Cousin's* glove!

She complimented him on the propriety of his behaviour
(Ryan). James I 'was pleased with his own Hand to write
an amicable Letter to Mr. *Shakespeare*; which Letter, tho
now lost, remained long in the Hands of Sir *William
D'avenant*' (Anon.). 'My Lord *Southampton*, at one time, gave
him a thousand Pounds, to enable him to go through with
a Purchase which he heard he had a mind to' (Rowe).

(6) *On Some Plays.* An intimate acquaintance of Shakespeare said that he had 'one of those chuckle-pated His-
torians for his particular Associate, that could scarce speak
a Word but upon that Subject; and he maintain'd him, or
he might have starv'd upon his History'. When Shakespeare wanted to write a History, he sent for him, and
took down heads for his purpose. 'Then with his natural
flowing Wit, he work'd it into all Shapes and Forms, as
his beautiful Thoughts directed' (Anon., 1728). *Titus
Andronicus* 'was not Originally his, but brought by a private
Author to be Acted, and he only gave some Master-touches
to one or two of the Principal Parts or Characters' (Ravenscroft). Of Mercutio in *Romeo and Juliet* Shakespeare said
himself 'that he was forced to kill him in the third Act,
to prevent being kill'd by him' (Dryden). 'In Shakespeares first show of Harrie the fifth, the person with which
he undertook to playe a buffone was not Falstaffe, but
Sir John Oldcastle, and offence beinge worthily taken by
Personages descended from his title, the poet was putt to
make an ignorant shifte of abusing Sir John Falstaffe'
(James). Here 'Harrie the fifth' is an error for *1, 2 Henry IV*,
where there are traces of Oldcastle, in the stage directions.

According to Sir William Bishop, 'part of Sir John Fal-staff's character was drawn from a townsman of Stratford, who either faithlessly broke a contract, or spitefully refused to part with some land for a valuable consideration, adjoining to Shakespeare's, in or near that town' (Oldys).

(7) *Shakespeare's Profits*. He 'supplied ye stage with 2 plays every year, and for y^t had an allowance so large, y^t he spent att a Rate of a 1,000*l*. a year' (Ward). 'He left 2 or 300^li per annum there and therabout to a sister' (Aubrey). He 'received but *five pounds* for his *Hamlet*; whether from the players who first acted it, or the printer or bookseller who first published it, is not distinguished' (Oldys). 'I thinke I have been told that he left 2 or 300^li per annum to a sister' (Aubrey). It was a sum of £20 with a house for life and his wearing apparel.

STRATFORD ONCE MORE

(1) *On the London Road*. 'He was wont to goe to his native County once a yeare' (Aubrey). 'The latter Part of his life was spent, as all Men of good Sense will wish theirs may be, in Ease, Retirement, and the Conversation of his Friends. He had the good Fortune to gather an Estate equal to his Occasion, and, in that to his Wish; and is said to have spent some years before his Death at his native *Stratford*. His pleasurable Wit, and good Nature, engag'd him in the Acquaintance, and entitled him to the Friendship of the Gentlemen of the Neighbourhood' (Rowe). 'Sir John Mennis saw once his old F*athe*r in his shop, a merry Cheekd old man, t*hat* s*ai*d, Will was a g*oo*d Hone*st* Fellow, but he durst h*av*e crackt a jeast with him at any time' (Plume). In fact Mennis was only born two years before John Shakespeare's death. Travelling between Stratford and London, Shakespeare is said to have stayed at the Crown Inn in Oxford, kept by John Daven-

ant, later Mayor of the town, and father of Sir William
Davenant (*n.* 1606), a Caroline poet and dramatist. A
very persistent tradition alleges that Sir William was in
fact a natural son of Shakespeare himself. Sir William's
'mother was a very beautiful woman, & of a very good
witt and of conversation extremely agreable. Mr. William
Shakespeare did commonly in his journey lye at this house
in Oxon: where he was exceedingly respected. I have
heard Parson Robert Davenant say that Mr. W. Shakespeare here gave him a hundred kisses. Now S^r W^m would
sometimes when he was pleasant over a glasse of wine with
his most intimate friends e.g. Sam: Butler (author of
Hudibras) &c. say, that it seemed to him that he writt
with the very spirit that Shakespeare, and was seemed
contented enough to be thought his Son: he would tell
them the story as above, in which way his mother had
a very light report, whereby she was called a whore'
(Aubrey). 'The father, who was a very grave and discreet
citizen (yet an admirer and lover of plays and play-makers,
especially Shakespeare, who frequented his house in his
journies between Warwickshire and London) was of a
melancholie disposition, and was seldom or never seen to
laugh' (Wood). A story of Shakespeare's relations with
the Earl of Southampton 'was handed down by Sir *William
Davenant*, who was probably very well acquainted with his
affairs' (Rowe). 'Mr. Shakespeare was Sir William's Godfather & gave him his name. (In all probability he got
him.) 'Tis further said that one day going from school a
grave Doctor in Divinity met him, and ask'd him, *Child,
whither art thou going in such hast?* to which the child reply'd,
*O Sir my Godfather is come to Town, & I am going to ask his
blessing.* To wch the Dr. said, *Hold Child, you must not take
the name of God in vaine'* (Hearne, also Oldys and Wight, with
variations). Davenant was supposed Shakespeare's 'natural

son' (Anon., 1748; Chetwood). But Oldys also says that the 'godfather' story, without the names of Shakespeare and Davenant, is told in the Works of John Taylor, the Water Poet (1630). One journey from London must have taken Shakespeare by another route than Oxford, for on it, at Grendon in Bucks., he found the humour of the Constable in *M.N.D.* (Aubrey). There is none. Probably Aubrey meant Dogberry in *Much Ado*.

(2) *Shakespeare's Houses.* 'I have been told that he writ the scene of the Ghost in *Hamlet*, at his House which bordered on the Charnel-House and Church-yard' (Gildon). Neither New Place nor the Birthplace was so situated. A mulberry planted by him was shown at the Birthplace (Anon., 1762). It was at New Place (Davenport, Sharp).

(3) *His Death.* 'He dyed a papist' (Davies). 'Shakespear, Drayton, and Ben Jhonson, had a merry meeting, and itt seems drank too hard, for Shakespear died of a feavour there contracted' (Ward). A Warwickshire gentleman 'had a wooden bench, once the favourite accommodation of Shakespeare, together with an earthen half-pint mug out of which he was accustomed to take his draughts of ale at a certain publick house in the neighbourhood of Stratford, every Saturday afternoon' (Steevens). 'My landlord, at a place called Bidford, shewed me in the hedge, a crab-tree, called Shakespear's Canopy, because under it our poet slept one night; for he, as well as Ben Johnson, loved a glass for the pleasure of society; and he, having heard much of the men of that village as deep drinkers and merry fellows, one day went over to Bidford, to take a cup with them. He enquired of a shepherd for the Bidford drinkers; who replied they were absent; but the Bidford sippers were at home; and, I suppose, continued the sheepkeeper, they will be sufficient for you: and so, indeed, they were. He was forced to take up his lodging

under that tree for some hours' (Anon., 1762, Jordan, with elaborations). Whether this is a story of his early or of his later days is not clear.

(4) *His Family*. He left a third daughter, besides Susanna and Judith (Rowe). He gave Double Falsehood 'as a Present of Value, to a natural Daughter of his, for whose Sake he wrote it, in the Time of his Retirement from the Stage' (Theobald). A baker of Warwick 'married one of the Descendants from *Shakespear*' (Roberts). 'Two young women, lineal descendants of our great dramatic poet' kept an alehouse, near Stratford and Bidford, in 1762 (Anon.). The epitaph on his tomb was 'made by himselfe a little before his Death.

> Good friend, for Jesus sake forbeare
> To digg the dust inclosed here
> Bles't be the man that spares these stones
> And Curs't be he that moves my bones!

Not one for feare of the Curse aboues^d Dare Touch his Grave Stone, tho his wife and Daughters Did Earnestly Desire to be Layd in the same Graue wth him' (Dowdall).

(5) *His Epigrams*. Visitors to Stratford could not escape being regaled with some sarcastic verses, said to have been written by Shakespeare on members of the Combe family. One, on John Combe, 'a noted usurer', was originally on his tomb, but was later razed by his heirs.

> Ten in the Hundred lies here ingrav'd,
> 'Tis a Hundred to Ten, his Soul is not sav'd:
> If any man ask, Who lies in this Tomb?
> Oh! ho! quoth the Devil, 'tis my John-a-Combe.

The other was on John's brother Thomas:

> Thin in beard and thick in purse;
> Never man beloved worse:
> He went to th' grave with many a curse:
> The Devil and He had both one nurse.

There are some variants (Hammond, Anon. 1650, Dobyns, Aubrey, Rowe, Peck, Macklin, Jordan). Thomas and John were respectively the father and uncle of the William Combe who was concerned with the Welcombe enclosure scheme in 1614. I should add that John's legacy of £5 to Shakespeare and Shakespeare's of his sword to Thomas's son discredit any idea of hostility between the families.

THE ATTITUDE TO TRADITION

WHAT then are we to think of tradition as an element in the making of a biography? It is obviously far less reliable than record, which may be misinterpreted, but at least gives a germ of fact, which has to be worked in at its appropriate place. Tradition is attractive. It may deal with more picturesque and intimate matter than record. On the other hand, it may be due to invention, either to decorate the dull narrative of a book or to satisfy the persistence of inquirers with tips in their pockets. In any case there is room for errors of transmission, either through inexact memories, or through the natural human instinct to leave a story better than you found it. Nevertheless, tradition cannot be altogether disregarded. A country neighbourhood is self-contained and tenacious of outstanding local personalities. An early visit to Stratford is recorded in 1630. It was by an anonym, who, although 'walking in the Church to do his devotion', tells us nothing of its object. Malone, in the preface to his edition of 1790, gives a list of long-lived persons who were likely to have authentic information about Shakespeare, and some of whom even Rowe might have consulted. Joan Hart lived to 1646, Susanna Hall to 1649, Judith Quiney to 1662, Lady Bernard to 1672, Sir John Bernard to 1674, Thomas

Combe the younger to 1657, William Combe the younger to 1667, Sir Richard Bishop of Bridgetown to 1672, his son Sir Nicholas Bishop, although only born in 1626, to 1700. The theatrical profession, again, was an hereditary caste, and traditions might readily be handed on. It is true that seventeenth-century actors, unlike modern ones of course, probably talked loosely in their cups.

Our attitude towards tradition must therefore be one, neither of credulity nor of complete scepticism, but of critical balance. There are criteria to be borne in mind. Does the tradition arise early or late? Does it come from more than one independent source? Does it help to explain record, or contradict it? Thus the tradition that Falstaff, as the name of a character, replaced Sir John Oldcastle, is confirmed by traces of Oldcastle's name in stage directions. But the statement that the Earl of Southampton gave Shakespeare £1,000 to make a purchase is inconsistent with our knowledge of his actual investments. Is there any reason to suspect deliberate falsehood? We know that William Henry Ireland was an habitual forger. A sexton, hoping for tips from inquirers, is not likely to be very scrupulous about what he tells them. Is the reporter likely to be reliable and well informed? John Aubrey was industrious and full of interest in antiquity, but inaccurate and given to scandal. John Ward, who tells of Shakespeare's death from a fever after drinking, had some medical knowledge.

Let us look at the Deer-stealing story, and that of the Bidford Crab-tree. The former emerges comparatively early, and from more than one source. It fits into Shakespeare's disappearance from Stratford records. On the other hand, the Justice Shallow theme in the *Merry Wives* might be its origin, rather than a reminiscence of it. Certainly its details have been elaborated in versions running on to the nineteenth century. Its locality has been shifted from park to park, in deference to historical criticism. The suggestion that the deer was taken to grace Shakespeare's marriage feast looks like an afterthought. The crab-tree story emerges nearly a century later in 1762. It is vague as to the date of the supposed event. It comes from the mouth of an innkeeper, suggesting a remunerative tour to a place some way from Stratford. Obviously its credentials are less good than those of the alleged deerstealing in its primitive form.

I think that perhaps the current attitude to tradition is rather inclined to err on the side of excessive scepticism. Thus Richard Davies tells us that Shakespeare died a Papist, and Sir Sidney Lee comments that 'we may dismiss as idle gossip the irresponsible report'. Now I do not know whether Shakespeare was ever, at any time of his life, a Papist. It perhaps fits in with the tone of his latest plays. But I am sure that Sir Sidney did not know anything about Davies which justified the assumption that he was irresponsible and given to idle gossip. He had been a Chaplain of my own college of Corpus Christi at Oxford and a friend of the learned collector of manuscripts, William Fulman. I found in the Bodleian a letter to him from Gilbert Burnet, the historian of the Reformation, in which Burnet says, 'I have not the honour to be known to you', and adds, 'I look upon you as one in whom our *Church* has great reason to *Glory*'. Probably he played some part, not yet disclosed, in the theological controversies of the Restoration. At any rate he was not a mere ignorant country parson, and may have known what he was writing about when he called Shakespeare a Papist. My advice to you then is to walk wary with Tradition. It is often a matter for an estimate of greater or less probability, rather than for confident assertion.

INFERENCES FROM SHAKESPEARE'S POEMS

ONE other topic we must consider. Is there anything in Shakespeare's non-dramatic writings which may yield us any information on his personal life? We have, of course, his two dedications of his *Venus and Adonis* in 1593 and *The Rape of Lucrece* in 1594 to Henry Wriothesley, Earl of Southampton. They are formal enough. There is nothing in the first to suggest any relation other than would naturally exist between a nobleman prominent at Court and a Court player. The second, with its references to 'the loue I dedicate to your Lordship' and 'the warrant I haue of your Honourable disposition' perhaps comes a little closer, but it is poor evidence for Southampton's alleged gift of £1,000.

Our only real hope must be in the *Sonnets*. These are full of personal hints, but the interpretation of them can only be conjectural. Francis Meres, in his *Palladis Tamia* of 1598, writes of Shakespeare's 'sugred Sonnets among his priuate friends', and describes him as one of those 'most passionate among us to bewaile and bemoane the perplexities of Loue'. In 1600 was registered for publication 'A booke called Amours by J. D. with certen Oy^r Sonnetes by W. S.' It is not extant, and we do not know whom the initials represent. The *Sonnets* we have were printed in 1609, and prefaced by a publisher's dedication which wishes 'To the onlie begetter of these insuing Sonnets Mr W. H. all happinesse and that eternitie promised by our ever-living poet'. They fall into two main groups. Those of the first (i–cxxvi) are all addressed to a boy-friend of the poet. He must clearly be the 'Mr W. H.' of the dedication. Its promise of eternity is in xviii.

> But thy eternall Sommer shall not fade,
> Nor loose possession of that faire thou ow'st,
> Nor shall death brag thou wandr'st in his shade,
> When in eternall lines to time thou grow'st.

But who was he? I do not think that any importance is to be attached to the line in xx,

> A man in hew all *Hews* in his controwling.

This has been held to point to an unknown Will Hughes, but the line is grammatically incorrect, and the most plausible correction, which substitutes 'a maiden hew', cannot be so interpreted. The first group of sonnets falls naturally into sub-groups. In the opening one of these the poet makes a continuous exhortation of his reluctant boy-friend to marriage. I myself feel little doubt that he was William Herbert, the son of the Earl of Pembroke, and this is confirmed by a recent discovery in the *Penshurst MSS.* that during 1595 an attempt to betroth Herbert to Elizabeth Carey, the daughter of Lord Hunsdon, the patron of Shakespeare's company, broke down, through Herbert's 'not liking'. The theme is not carried on into the remaining sub-groups, which deal respectively with the poet's love for his friend and self-depreciation (xiii–xxxii), the fault of the friend, who has taken a mistress from him (xxxiii–xlii), the endurance of love in absence (xliii–lxvi), the friend's faults and slanders to which they expose him (lxvii–lxx), the poet's growing age and fidelity (lxxi–lxxvii), the attraction of a rival poet for the youth, through 'the proud full sail of his great verse' (lxxviii–lxxxvi), the poet's faults (lxxxvii–xci), his friend's faults (xcii–xcvi), the renewal of affection (c–cviii), the frailty of the poet, who has on his side been faithless (cix–cxxi), a final assertion that Love conquers Time (cxxii–cxxv), a final *Envoi* to the 'lovely boy'. It appears from civ that the friendship had lasted for a period of three years, when that was written. I take them to run from the autumn of 1595 to the autumn of 1598. In cvii we get:

> The mortall Moone hath her Eclipse indur'de,
> And the sad Augurs mock their owne presage,
> Incertenties now crown them-selues assur'de,
> And peace proclaimes Oliues of endlesse age.

This must, I think, date from the end of 1599 or beginning of 1600, when a rumour that Elizabeth was dead or dangerously ill had been dispelled, and a prospect of peace with Spain seemed to be opening.

There may be some confirmation of intimacy between Shakespeare and William Herbert in a note by William Cory (1865, *Diary*) of a letter at Wilton House, bidding Herbert bring James I to a performance of *As You Like It* there. 'We have the man Shakespeare with us', she wrote. No trace of this letter could be found in 1898. But the Court was at Wilton in October–December 1603.

The second group of sonnets (cxxvii–clii) is undatable, but was not necessarily written later than the first. The poet has taken a woman 'collour'd ill', with raven black eyes. She has broken her bed-vow in loving him, and then torn her new faith by making his sweetest friend a slave to slavery. It is possible therefore that she is the woman of xxxiii–xlii, although there is no reference to blackness in those. There is much word-play on 'Will' and 'will':

> Who euer hath her wish, thou hast thy *Will*,
> And Will too boote, and Will in ouer-plus,
> More then enough am I that vexe thee still,
> To thy sweet will making addition thus.

One other document must be cited which may have some relation to the *Sonnets*. In September 1594 was published *Willobie His Avisa*, which records the love affair with a girl called Avisa of one Henry Willoughby, a Wiltshire man by birth, and sometime an Oxford student. With most of this we are not concerned, but the following passage is interesting.

H. W. being sodenly infected with the contagion of a fantasticall fit, at the first sight of *A*, pyneth a while in secret griefe, at length not able any longer to indure the burning heate of so feruent a humour, bewrayeth the secresy of his disease vnto his familiar frend W. S. who not long before had tryed the curtesy of the like passion, and was now newly recouered of the like infection; yet finding his frend let bloud in the same vaine, he took pleasure for a tyme to see him bleed, & in steed of stopping the issue, he inlargeth the wound, with the sharpe rasor of a willing conceit, perswading him that he thought it a matter very easy to be compassed, & no doubt with payne, diligence & some cost in time to be obtayned. Thus this miserable comforter comforting his frend with an impossibilitie, either for that he now would secretly laugh at his frends folly, that had giuen occasion not long before vnto others to laugh at his owne, or because he would see whether an other could play his part better then himselfe, & in vewing a far off the course of this louing Comedy, he determined to see whether it would sort to a happier end for this new actor, then it did for the old player.

A verse dialogue follows, which adds nothing, except for a couplet:

> She is no Saynt, She is no Nonne,
> I thinke in tyme she may be wonne.

This perhaps echoes *Titus Andronicus*, II. i. 82–3.

> She is a woman, therefore may be woo'd;
> She is a woman, therefore may be won.

On the whole I think that W. S. is probably Shakespeare, although 'the old player' here is not necessarily a technical term. His intrigue with the dark lady may quite well have begun as early as 1594. It is not important that the passage in *Willobie His Avisa* does not tell us whether the woman concerned was a brunette or not. Some fresh light has recently come from Professor Leslie Hotson, who points out in his *I, William Shakespeare* (1937) that Henry Willoughby was connected, through a marriage of his brother, with the Russells of Strensham, one of whom, Thomas Russell, who had the manor of Alderminster on the road from Stratford to Oxford and London, was nominated by Shakespeare as an overseer of his will.

SOME FINAL HINTS

WE have done with Shakespeare. Let us remember that we have taken him as the subject of these lectures, not so much for his own sake, than as typical. Let me wind up with a few hints which might help you in entering for the first time upon other regions of biographical research.

Part of your equipment must be as close a knowledge as you can get of how institutions worked in their relation to the individuals affected by them. Records must be read with an understanding of the purposes for which they were written, and the only facts you must expect to find in them are those relevant to such purposes. Take for example Shakespeare's will. Surprise has been expressed that it makes no mention of books, and the inference drawn that he can have possessed none. And again that he names no legacies to his wife. He must have quarrelled with her. But the object of a will is to transfer property, although it is true that in Elizabethan days some expression of piety was usual, before you tried to tie up as closely as possible the property of which you were reluctantly losing control; and that some testators, then and since, have made their wills an occasion for manifestoes of their dislike of taxation or their displeasure with relatives. Such books as Shakespeare possessed would pass with his other chattels. If they were enumerated, it would be in an inventory, lost in this case, not in the body of the will itself. Similarly, his widow was legally entitled to her dower during lifetime of a third of his lands and houses. It was not necessary to express this in the will, although it was sometimes done. His bequest to her of his 'second-best bed' reads as if it were depreciatory, but it probably was not. Similar bequests occur in other contemporary wills, in that of Thomas Combe, for example. The best bed was often an heirloom, and Shakespeare's heir was his daughter, not his wife.

Here are a few points of practical advice.

(1) Do not be content with the second-hand statements of modern writers when you can get at the original sources.

(2) Absorb such contemporary documents as are in print before starting on manuscripts. This will both give you clues and save you the disappointment of discovering what has been discovered before.

(3) Get a thorough knowledge of handwriting during the period with which you are concerned. You will, no doubt, have separate lectures on this. Of course some records, especially legal ones, are in Latin. But you cannot do much good in research, at any early date, without Latin.

(4) Familiarize yourself with some catches of chronology. Early documents are often dated not by calendar years, but by the regnal years of the Sovereign. Keep at your elbows one of the various convenient handbooks, such as W. D. Selby's *Jubilee Date-Book* (1887), which gives these.

(5) Remember that, in Elizabethan times, the New Year was generally (not, I fear, invariably) regarded as

beginning, not on January 1, but on Annunciation Day, March 25.

(6) Remember that in 1582 Pope Gregory XIII cut ten days out of the calendar for that year. I need not go into his reasons. But the change, although accepted at once by Italy, France, Spain, the Netherlands, and other Catholic countries, was not adopted by Great Britain until 1752, with the result that for a long period English and Continental datings were not in agreement. If you do not bear this in mind you may be sometimes puzzled by finding that a letter from abroad appears to be answered on a date earlier than its own.

(7) Some writers do not always date their letters fully, but a reference in a letter to some contemporary event, of which the date is known, will often help you.

(8) A perpetual calendar, such as H. Grotefend's *Taschenbuch der Zeitrechnung* (1898), showing on which day of the week every calendar date fell, is a great convenience.

BIBLIOGRAPHICAL NOTE

MOST of the Records, Contemporary Allusions, and Traditions considered in these Lectures are to be found in my *William Shakespeare* (1930). Some additional notes on the *Sonnets* are in my *Shakespearean Gleanings* (1944).

A *Shakespeare Bibliography* (1931) is edited by W. Ebisch and L. L. Schücking. A Supplement (1937) covers the years 1930 to 1935. Current work on Shakespeare is considered in *The Year's Work in English Studies* (English Association), of which volumes for 1919–42 have so far been published. A wider range is that of A. W. Pollard and G. R. Redgrave, *A Short-Title Catalogue of Books Printed in England, Scotland and Ireland, and of English Books Printed Abroad in 1475–1640* (1926); and of W. W. Greg in *English Literary Autographs, 1550–1650* (1925), and in *Dramatic Documents from the Elizabethan Playhouses*, with *A Commentary* (1931), and *A Bibliography of the English Printed Drama to the Restoration* (1939, vol. i, *Stationers Records*, 1475 to 1616).

Some useful writings, of later date than that of my *William Shakespeare*, are J. W. Mackail, *The Approach to Shakespeare* (1930), H. Granville-Barker, *Prefaces to Shakespeare* (1927, 1930, 1937), F. Marcham, *Shakespeare and His Family* (1931), *The Shakespeare Allusion Book* (new ed. 1932), J. Dover Wilson, *The Essential Shakespeare* (1932), G. B. Harrison, *Shakespeare at Work* (1933), H. Granville-Barker and G. B. Harrison, with others, *A Companion to Shakespeare Studies* (1934), C. F. E. Spurgeon, *Shakespeare's Imagery and What It Tells Us* (1935), Irvine Gray, 'Shakespeare's Son-in-Law' (1936, *Genealogist's Magazine*), P. Alexander, *Shakespeare's Life and Art* (1939), M. Van Doren, *Shakespeare* (1939), H. Spencer, *The Art and Life of William Shakespeare* (1940).

Students of lives other than that of Shakespeare will find material in the Public Record Office, with the help of *List Q*, supplied by the Office itself, of the official *Guide* by M. S. Giuseppi (1923–4), and of V. H. Galbraith, *An Introduction to the Use of the Public Records* (1934); in the Reports of the *Historical Manuscripts Commission*, especially those on the muniments of the Earl of Salisbury at Hatfield, of Lord De L'Isle and Dudley at Penshurst (to be supplemented by A. Collins, *Letters and Memorials of State*, 1746), of the Duke of Buccleugh at Montagu House, London (to be supplemented by E. Sawyer, *Memorials of Affairs of State in the Reigns of Queen Elizabeth and King James I*, 1725), and of the

Duke of Rutland at Belvoir; in the *Acts of the Privy Council* from 1386 to 1617, edited successively by H. Nicolas, J. R. Dasent, and H. C. Maxwell-Lyte with J. V. Lyle; in the *Calendars of State Papers* from 1547 onwards; in the *Reports on the Transcription and Publication of Parish Registers*, and the *Index of Archaeological Papers*, issued by the Congress of Archaeological Societies and the Society of Antiquaries; and in G. W. Cole, *Index to Bibliographical Papers Published by the Bibliographical Society and the Library Association* (1933).

Valuable treatises and lists are C. Gross, *A Bibliography of British Municipal History* (1897) and *The Sources and Literature of English History from the Earliest Times to about 1485* (1900); W. Rye, *Records and Record Searching* (ed. 2, 1897); F. P. Barnard, *Companion to English History in the Middle Ages* (1902); N. J. Hone, *The Manor and Manorial Records* (1906); H. Hall, *Studies in English Official Historical Documents* (1908); R. H. Gretton, *The King's Government* (1913); *Helps for Students of History* (S.P.C.K. 1918 seqq.).

INDEX